A Journey through
Mark's Gospel

By

Marjorie Farrell Morley

Print Origination (NW) Limited
Formby, Merseyside L37 8EG

Contents

Index covering all sixteen chapters
Who was Mark?..30
The Sadducees...30
The Sanhedrin..32
The Pharisees..32
The Scribes or Teachers of the Law...............................32
The Herodians...33
The Gentiles..33
Explanation of Parable and Allegory..............................34
Meaning of Covenant..36
Meaning of Gospel..36
The Explanation of the Gospel verses according to Mark
Chapter One..38
Chapter Two..52
Chapter Three...64
Chapter Four...72
Chapter Five..82
Chapter Six...93
Chapter Seven...106
Chapter Eight...115
Chapter Nine..126
Chapter Ten..135
Chapter Eleven...146
Chapter Twelve...155
Chapter Thirteen..164
Chapter Fourteen...172
Chapter Fifteen..193
Chapter Sixteen...207
The Kingdom of God..216
Discipleship..219
Jesus in Mark's Gospel..223
Opposition and Conflict...232
Questions..237
Key Quotations...240

First published in 1993 by
Print Origination (NW) Limited
Formby
Merseyside L37 8EG

ISBN 0 903348 42 X

Illustrations throughout by F. Sumner

Typeset and produced by
Print Origination (NW) Ltd., Formby, Liverpool L37 8EG
Printed and bound in Britain

Introduction

The contents of this book provide a practical approach to the person and ministry of Jesus, according to Mark's Gospel. The book has been carefully planned to enable pupils of all abilities to find easy access to material relevant to their G.C.S.E. course. Questions will be found at the end of each chapter, and at the back of the book. They cover the objectives for G.C.S.E., knowledge, understanding, and evaluation. The aims of this book are to enrich the lives of the reader, stimulate interest, and give a clearer understanding of Mark's Gospel, which will be assessed under the criteria for G.C.S.E. Religious Studies.

It also aims to establish that Christ is the centre of all Christian lives. His work continues within us through the strength and guidance of the Holy Spirit.

The index is to be found at the beginning of the book which covers the individual chapters. It includes a separate section for parables and miracles with reference to chapter and verse. This is followed by an explanation of biblical terms. The book should be used in conjunction with the Bible because it explains chapter and verse throughout. Pupils need their own copy of this book when they are studying the gospel either at home, or at school. The teacher can direct the pupils, after reading a text, both in discussion and set work. It will enable the pupil not only to express knowledge and understanding, but enrich their ability to evaluate the scriptures. This book also provides easy access to the topics that will be covered in coursework. In addition it would be of value to 'A' level students studying the 'New Testament Studies', and to those seeking to understand what Jesus is saying to the world.

Foreword

There is a great need for the gospels to be presented to students in clear, simple language, so that the message of Jesus is truly heard by His audiences today. M.M. goes a long way to achieve this goal. She takes the student line by line through the text while sparing them the difficulties that might "turn them off."

The message comes across as immediate and clear. M.M. sets up a dialogue between the student and the text that must make it easier for the teacher to bring the student into praying the Scriptures, and so experiencing its grace.

Ultimately the gospels were written, not just to be studied but to be lived, so that the reader becomes a disciple, and therefore a follower of Jesus. The text must not be dealt with as a "dead letter" but as the "Living Word". I sincerely hope that all who journey through St. Mark with M.M. will also begin the great adventure of following Jesus, and knowing in their personal experience that He is the Life.

Frances Hogan

Dedication

I dedicate this book to David and Philip, and to all the youth. May they always walk with God, and love and serve Him faithfully.

To my Sisters in Christ, His beloved disciples, Sister M. Yvonne, O.S.A., and Frances Hogan. May their 'Light of Christ' be an example to us all.

To Ann, Damien and Stephen, R.I.P. They walked through life as examples of young Christian love and fervour for God. They walked into His arms and to eternal happiness.

> "We are told to sing to the Lord a new song.
> A new man knows a new song.
> A song is a thing of joy and if we think of it,
> a thing of love.
> So the man who has learned to have a new life
> has learned to sing a new song.
> For a new man, a new song and the New Testament
> all belong to the same Kingdom."
> St. Augustine

Acknowledgements

I would like to thank the following people whose help and support have greatly assisted the publication of this book.
Mr and Mrs E. Jackson, Sr. M. Yvonne O.S.A., The Advent Trust, Mr and Mrs R. Bird, Mr T. Clarke, Mr and Mrs A Dawber, Mrs A Farrell, Dr and Mrs M. J. King, Mr and Mrs F. Maxey, Mr and Mrs F. Sumner, Mr P. L. Bryan, Mr T. Morley and Mr P. R. Withers.

"When I needed a neighbour you were there."

Frances Hogan, scripture treacher and author, for her inspiration and teachings on Mark's Gospel.

My grateful thanks to The British and Foreign Bible Society for:
Scriptures quoted from the Good News Bible
published by The Bible Societys/Harper Collins Publishers Ltd., UK
American Bible Society, 1966, 1971, 1976, 1992,

Chapter One

V1-8	John the Baptist	Beginning of the Gospel Preached Repentance	River Jordan
V9-11	Baptism of Jesus	Identifies himself with the people	
		Jesus brings the Good News	
V12-13	Temptations	Jesus was tested 'Pure Gold'	
V14-15	Preached	Started his Public Ministry	Galilee
V16-20	Call of Disciples	Need of friends to help in his work	Lake Galilee
V21-28	Evil Spirit	They recognised Jesus but men did not	Capernaum
V29-31	Peter's Mother-in-Law	Miracle	Capernaum
V32-34	Cures the Sick Casts out Demons	Healing of 'many' Plays down role of Messiah	Capernaum
V35-39	Departure Preaches in	Speaks with his Father	Galilee
	Synagogues Drives out Demons	Continues his Father's work	
V40-45	Cures a Leper	Miracle	Galilee

Chapter Two

V1-5	Paralytic Forgiveness	Miracle Great Faith	Capernaum
V6-12	Blasphemy	Conflict with Pharisees Miracle of Forgiveness	Capernaum
V13-14	Calls Levi	Heavenly wealth	Lake Galilee
V15-17	Eats with Sinners	Conflict with Pharisees	Galilee
V18-20	Question of Fasting	Conflict with Pharisees	Galilee
V21-22	Patches and Wine Skins	Conflict with Pharisees	Galilee
V23-28	Question about the Sabbath	Conflict with Pharisees	Galilee

Chapter Three

V1-6	The Sabbath The Man with Paralysed Hand	Conflict with Pharisees and Herodians They plan to kill Jesus	Synagogue Galilee
V7-12	Healing of the Crowds	No time to eat and rest Preaches from the boat	Lake Galilee
V13-19	Twelve Apostles Appointed	Twelve tribes in the old Israel	Galilee
V20-21	Anxiety of Relatives	Heard stories out of context	They come to Galilee
V22	Beelzebul Charge	Pharisees charge Jesus	Galilee
V23-30	Parables on Satan The Unforgivable Sin	Jesus speaks in Parables To say Jesus is possessed by Satan	Galilee
V31-35	Who are my Relatives?	Those who do God's will	Galilee

Chapter Four
Parables

V1-9	Parable of the Sower	Speaks about Faith	Taught from boat on Lake Galilee
V10-12	Purpose of the Parables	Everyone must be given the chance to accept or reject	Galilee
V13-20	Explanation of Sower	A good or bad harvest	Galilee
V21-25	Lamp and Measure	Faith Let it grow	Galilee
V26-29	The Growing Seed	Give yourself to God	Galilee
V30-34	The Mustard Seed	Power of God is made perfect in your weakness	Galilee
V35-41	Jesus calms the storm	Miracle Faith	Crossing Lake Galilee

Chapter Five

Miracles

V1-20	Man with Evil Spirits	Man's blindness Satan hates to lose territory	The other side of lake
V21-24	Jairus	Aware of the power of Jesus	Returned across lake
V25-34	The Sick Women	Faith	Galilee
V35-43	Healing of Jairus' Daughter	Compassion of Jesus	Galilee

Chapter Six

V1-6	Jesus is Rejected	No Faith	Nazareth
V7-13	The Twelve Go Out	Miracles	Villages around Nazareth
V14-29	Death of John the Baptist	Due to pride and the lust of two women	Galilee
V30-44	Feeding of the 5,000	Miracle	Galilee
V45-52	Jesus Walks on the Water	Miracle	Lake Galilee
V53-56	Jesus Heals the Sick	Miracles	Gennesaret

Chapter Seven

V1-5	Jewish Rituals	Conflict with Pharisees	Galilee Gennesaret
V6-13	The Corban	Fourth Commandment	Galilee Gennesaret
V14-23	Teaching on being unclean	Your Heart	Galilee Gennesaret
V23-30	Syro-Phoenician Women	Faith Miracle Healed from a distance	Near Tyre
V31-37	Jesus Heals a Deaf Mute	Miracle	Outside Galilee

Chapter Eight

V1-10	Second Loaves	Miracle	Outside Galilee
V11-13	Pharisees ask for a Miracle	Miracle	Dalmanutha
V14-21	Influence of Herod and Pharisees	Warning	On the lake
V22-26	The Blind Man	Miracle	Bethsaida
V27-30	Peter's confession of Faith	Hinge Question Messiahship	Villages near Caesarea Philippi
V31-33	First Prophecy of Passion	Teaching on Messiahship	Villages near Caesarea Philippi
V34-38	True Discipleship	Teaching	Villages near Caesarea Philippi

Chapter Nine

V1-10	The Transfiguration	Means change of appearance	Probably Mount Hermon
V11-13	The Coming of Elijah	Teaching on Messiahship	Probably Mount Hermon
V14-29	Boy with an Evil Spirit	Need of Faith!	Down from Mount Hermon
V30-32	Second Prophecy of Passion	Teaching on Messiahship	Through Galilee
V33-37	Who is the Greatest	Being God's Servant	Capernaum
V38-41	Whoever is not against Us is for Us	Using the name of Jesus Predudice–Discrimination	Capernaum
V42-50	Temptations to Sin	Cut sin out of your life Discipleship	Capernaum

Here Jesus' Galilean Ministry comes to an end

Chapter Ten

On the way to Jerusalem

Jesus makes his way from the north down to Jericho on his journey to Jerusalem

V1-12	Teaches about Divorce	Pharisees try to trap him	Crossed the Jordan on the way to Jerusalem
V13-16	Jesus Blesses the Children	Innocence	Crossed the Jordan
V17-22	The Rich Man	All your security in money Ten Commandments	Commences his journey to Jerusalem
V23-31	Dangers in Riches	Put your security in God	Commences his journey to Jerusalem
V32-34	Third Teaching on Passion	Teaching on Messiahship	Road up to Jerusalem
V35-40	The Request of James and John	They do not realise what they are asking	Road up to Jerusalem
V41-45	Gave His Life to Redeem	Man must serve	Road up to Jerusalem
V46-52	Blind Bartimaeus	Faith Miracle	Jericho

Chapter Eleven

Holy Week

Palm Sunday

V1-11	Entry into Jerusalem	Messiahship	Went to Bethany

Monday

V12-14	Jesus Curses the Fig Tree	Israel Bore no fruit Only time Jesus passes judgement	Coming back from Bethany
V15-17	Jesus goes to the Temple	Reverence in my Father's House Cleansing Discrimination	Jerusalem
V18-19	Heard of Temple Cleansing	Chief Priests plot to kill Jesus	Jerusalem
V20-25	Lesson from the Fig Tree	Judaism is dead	Jerusalem

Tuesday

V27-33	Question on Jesus' Authority	Jesus turns the question on them. Opposition	Jerusalem

Chapter Twelve

V1-12	Parable of the Tenants in the Vineyard	Obviously aimed at the Pharisees	Jerusalem
V13-17	Paying Taxes to Caesar	Trap Question Pharisees	Jerusalem
V18-27	Rising from the Dead	Trap Question Sadducees	Jerusalem
V28-34	The Great Commandment	Trap Question	Jerusalem
V35-37	Question about the Messiah	Jesus asks a question	Jerusalem
V38-40	Warnings against Scribes	Public warning by Jesus	Jerusalem
V41-44	The Widow's Offering	Put her religion into practice	Jerusalem

A Journey through Mark's Gospel

Chapter Thirteen

V1-2	Destruction of the Temple	Time of great sorrow	Jerusalem
V3-13	Troubles and Persecutions	Persecution and deception	Mount of Olives
V14-23	The Awful Horror	Put the standard of the Roman Legion into the Holy of Holies	Jerusalem
V24-27	The Coming of the Son of Man	The second coming	Jerusalem
V28-31	Lesson of the Fig Tree	God is near	Jerusalem
V32-37	No One knows the Day or Hour	Stay alert	Jerusalem

Chapter Fourteen

Wednesday

V1-2	The Plot Against Jesus	Premeditated Murder	Jerusalem
V3-9	Anointing at Bethany	Great reverence Act of Love	Bethany
V10-11	Judas Betrays Jesus	Why?	Jerusalem

Thursday

V12-21	Passover Meal with Disciples	Prophecy of betrayal	Jerusalem
V22-26	The Lord's Supper	Going to feed his Church for all time	Jerusalem
V27-31	Peter's denial	Peter's weakness	Jerusalem
V32-42	Gethsemane	Great anguish and suffering Humanity of Jesus	Jerusalem
V43-52	The Arrest of Jesus	Warning	Jerusalem
V53-65	Jesus before the Council	An illegal meeting	Jerusalem
V66-72	Peter Denies Jesus	Prophecy came true	Jerusalem

Chapter Fifteen

V1-5	Jesus is brought before Pilate	Fulfilling Roman rules	Jerusalem
V6-15	Sentenced to death	Innocence takes the place of Guilt	Jerusalem
V16-20	Crowning with Thorns	Suffered horrific pain	Jerusalem
V21-32	Crucifixion	Died to save mankind	Golgotha
V33-41	Death of Jesus	Fulfilled his Father's will	Golgotha
V42-47	The Burial	Joseph of Arimathea	Golgotha

Chapter Sixteen

V1-8	The Resurrection	"God is the God of the Living"	Jerusalem
V9-11	Apparition to Mary Magdalene	Mary told the others	Jerusalem
V12-13	Apparition to Two Disciples	Appeared as a traveller	Jerusalem
V14-18	Apparition to the Eleven	Reaction was fantastic	Jerusalem
V19-20	The Ascension	Jesus sits with his Father	Jerusalem

Parables

Chapter

2:V21   New Cloth and New Wine – Judaism is Dead – New Covenant

4:V1-9   The Parable of the Sower – The Kingdom of God – Allegory

V13-20   The Parable of the Sower – The Kingdom of God – Growth

4:V26   The Parable of the Growing Seed – The Kingdom of God – Growth

4:V30   The Mustard Seed – The Kingdom of God – Growth

4:V21   The Lamp under a Bowl – Good News Will Spread in the World – Hidden Faith

4:V24   The Measure – Judging Others – God is Our Judge

11:V12-14 Jesus Curses the Fig Tree – Judaism is Dead – No Fruit

11:V20-26 Lesson From the Fig Tree – Have Faith

12:V1   Tenants in the Vineyard – Jewish Relationship with God – Allegory

13:V28   Lesson of the Fig Tree – The Coming of Christ is Near – Warning

13:V33   The Absent Householder – Be Ready for the Coming of Christ – Warning

Miracles

Chapter	Attributed to Sickness		Healed By
1:V30	Peter's Mother-in-Law Fever		Touch: Sabbath
1:V40	The Leper		Touch
2:V3	The Paralysed Man Also Sin		Words: Faith: Authority
3:V1	Man with Paralysed Hand		Words: Sabbath Authority
5:V25	Woman with a Haemorrhage		Touch: Faith
5:V22-35	Jairus' Daughter Dead		Touch: Aramaic Words
7:V32	The Deaf and Dumb Man		Touch: Aramaic Words
8:V22	The Blind Man at Bethsaida		Touch
10:V46	Blind Bartimaeus		Words: Faith

	Attributed to Evil		
1:V23	A Man with an Evil Spirit		Words: Authority Sabbath
5:V2	A Man with Evil Spirits (Pigs)		Words: Authority
7:V25	The Syro-Phoenician Daughter	Foreigner and Gentile	Distance: Faith
9:V17	The Epileptic Boy		Words: Authority Need For Faith

	Attributed to Nature		
4:V35	Jesus Calms a Storm		Power: Words
6:V30	Jesus Feeds 5,000 Men		Power: 'Gave thanks to God'
6:V45	Jesus Walks on the Water		Power
8:V1	Jesus Feeds 4,000 People		Power: 'Gave thanks to God'
9:V2	The Transfiguration		Power
11:V12-14 V20-26	Jesus Curses the Fig Tree		Power: Words

Who was Mark?

Scholars believe Mark to be a disciple and not an apostle. We know that later still he is a disciple of Peter and in fact it is accepted that the teaching in the Gospel of St. Mark is that of the Gospel of Peter.

It is said that his Mother, Mary, had a 'House of Prayer' in Jerusalem and that many early Christians would gather there (Acts 12: 12).

Mark in his Gospel presents Jesus as a Servant "Behold my Servant" (Isaiah 42: 1). You see Jesus here in his humblest role.

This is the Gospel of the worker. This is Jesus, the workman, the servant of God, sent to represent his Father and to found the Kingdom of his Father, in his Father's name. He is God's representative on Earth.

Mark writes his Gospel about AD 65 during a time of Great Persecution for Christians. No doubt it brings comfort and greater understanding of their sufferings as they meditate upon the words and works of Jesus, their King and their **Saviour**.

The Sadducees

They come from the Priestly Families of Jerusalem. They are a powerful group of men who hold high positions of authority at the time of Jesus. Not only does their power and authority come through religion, but they act as local officials for the Roman Government.

Many of them are Jewish aristocrats and they are given power by the Romans to have authority over the Jewish people. Therefore they are a religious party and also a political party. They lose favour with the ordinary Jews because of their dealings with the Romans.

In the Gospel of Mark, they are mentioned during Jesus' trial because they have some influence over legal affairs. The High Priest is not only the leader but also the Chairman of the Sanhedrin.

Their main concern is centred on the Temple in Jerusalem which is

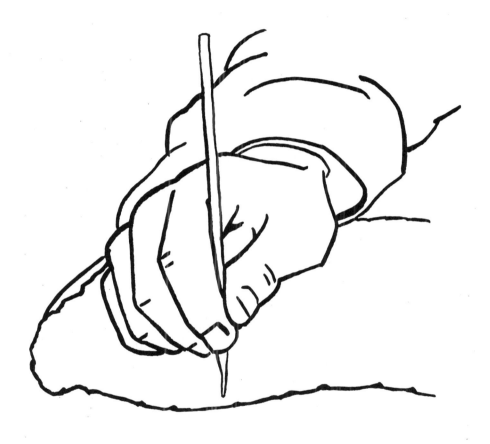

the centre of the Jewish religion. Therefore the Sadducees are in strict control over religious practice and affairs. They keep to the Law of Moses but refuse to believe in a life after death, in angels or spirits.

The Sanhedrin

This is the highest court of law for the Jewish people. The Council is made up of Sadducees and Pharisees. They use a room in the temple for court proceedings.

The Pharisees

We hear a great deal about the Pharisees in the Gospel of Mark. We find that they are in conflict and opposition with Jesus on many occasions. The name Pharisee means 'separated one'. Why? Because their aim in life is to separate themselves from anything that will make them unclean or lead them into sin. This is one reason why they will not mix with Pagans or Romans. They follow the rules and Laws from the Old Testament. They also keep the unwritten laws, teachings passed down orally which became known as the 'oral tradition'.

They keep to the rules and rituals of the Jewish religion, attend services in the Temple and fast. Unlike the Sadducees they believe in a life after death, in angels or spirits.

They are not Priests, but devout people with a great deal of influence and power. Many are members of the Sanhedrin.

Some are religious teachers and they are called Rabbis. Jesus is called Rabbi meaning 'teacher'. Jesus finds that they have lost sight of their aim to be holy and serve God. This is because they keep too rigidly to rules, such as how to wash, how and what to eat, which resulted in great conflict. Their religion has become far too legalistic!

The Scribes or Lawyers

Here we find another group of people in Mark's Gospel who are in conflict with Jesus.

They are extremely well educated and became experts in the Scriptures and writings of the Jewish religion. They are the interpreters of the Law by which the people lived.

The power and respect they held is for their work as writers and interpreters of the sacred books of the bible. They train for many years studying the scrolls of the Old Testament and learning how to teach the Law to the ordinary Jew. They spend their lives reading and studying the Old Testament to find the exact meaning of the words of God.

Obviously they are considered very important people within the Jewish Society, but they are poor because they receive little money for their work.

A Scribe will make a scroll to write on from sheepskin and papyrus reeds and use a thin reed as a pen. The ink is made from soot, gum and water which is mixed together.

The Herodians

They are a Jewish Political Group who support Herod Antipas, ruler of Galilee. Herod Antipas has John the Baptist's head cut off. It is said that he has his Jewish wife and two young sons murdered. He is a very immoral man and is the Son of Herod who has all the male babies killed at the time of the birth of Jesus.

To support this man reflects the followers that they are known to be, immoral and very indifferent to their religion.

The Gentiles

The name Gentile is given by the Jews to foreigners, such as the Romans or Greeks. The Jews hate their Roman rulers, not only because they are gentiles, but because they worship Pagan Gods. Jewish rules and regulations keep them away from Gentiles as much as possible. The Jews consider the Gentile as an un-Godly person. If they come in contact with a Gentile due to trading, they will have to wash themselves 'clean' when they get home. They are not allowed to enter a Gentile home or sit down and eat with them. You will find that Jesus does not keep these rules and regulations. In fact he enters their homes, eat with them and preaches to them. Many Gentiles become followers of Jesus and see the 'light' before the Jews do!

Parable and Allegory

Jesus is the 'Master Teacher'. He uses the simplest illustrations and the smallest words to get across God's message to his people.

A parable is an illustration of truth. Therefore Jesus uses the things of his time to help people understand. He uses outdoor life, the farmer sowing his seed, fish, nature and bread. He illustrates with anything that the ordinary people have experience of. The word parable comes from the Greek word *Parabola* which means that when you put two things side by side, it will illustrate what you are trying to say. There are two forms of parables, the simple, and the allegorical.

The simple parable is shown in the 'Lamp under a Bowl'. Here Jesus is saying that we should not hide our faith, but let it shine like a light within our lives, so that others may see.

The allegorical parables are stories in which one subject is used to bring another to mind. Some parables have allegorical details in which each point of the parable will have a specific meaning. Many parables have one point only.

In Mark there are only two allegorical parables, 'The Sower' and 'The Tenants in the Vineyard'.

The parable of 'The Sower' is explained in Chapter Four [The seed = The word of God].

The parable of 'The Tenants in the Vineyard', is explained in Chapter Twelve [Vineyard = Israel, God's people].

Parables stimulate your thoughts, they make you think. Jesus even has the courage to attack the religious policy of the Jews in the 'Tenants in the Vineyard' parable. That is why after listening to many of his parables they want to kill him.

Parables are meant to summarise the teachings of Jesus and to make it clear to us that we should search for the truth. We should realise that the Gospel message, the parables, are not just for the people of Jesus' time, they are for you and me; HERE and NOW!

Therefore we should pray to God and ask him to give us the eyes to see and the ears to hear, His words.

A Covenant

A covenant is an agreement or contract. God makes an agreement with his people at different stages through history. A covenant always has a sign. The first covenant that God makes with man is Noah and the sign is the rainbow. This is to be an everlasting sign.

God says that it will be an everlasting Covenant. We also know that the world will never end by a flood. (Genesis 9: 12—17. God's second Covenant is with Abraham. He says "Each one must be circumcised, and this will be a physical sign to show that my Covenant with you is everlasting" (Genesis 17: 13).

The third Covenant is made with Moses on Mount Sinai. It is here that God gave the *Ten Commandments* for the Jewish people to live by.

Because man did not keep these Covenants but turned to evil ways, God sent his only Son, Jesus.

Jesus makes the Greatest Covenant of all time with man. He makes the *New Covenant* and the sign is to be his very own blood which is shed for the *Salvation* of all mankind.

The Gospel

The word comes from an Anglo-Saxon word meaning 'God-Spel'. It is the story of the good news about God, which Jesus brought for all mankind to hear. It is passed on to the disciples of Jesus to preach to all nations. The four Gospel writers, Matthew, Mark, Luke and John have written down all that they have seen and heard. They want to preserve what Jesus has said and done for all future generations. The Gospels are written in Greek which is the language of the day.

However, Jesus speaks Aramaic and we find Aramaic words in Chapters Five, Seven and Fifteen.

St. Mark Chapter One

'John the Baptist'

V1   Here we have Mark introducing Jesus right at the beginning of the Gospel, but he never mentions the genealogy of Jesus. This is because he wants to show the lowly role of Jesus, the *Servant Role*. Servants do not have family trees drawn up because they are not considered important enough.

V2   He mentions the prophet Isaiah's teachings. The 'Messenger' is John the Baptist who will instruct the people in preparation for the coming of the 'Lord'.

V3   The 'Lord', is Jesus, the Christ. Christ is *Christos* in Greek and Messiah is Hebrew. They both mean 'The Anointed One.'
       When Jesus comes, Israel literally is a wilderness. It lay in the darkness of sin, but Jesus brings light into the darkness of Satan.
       "The word was the Source of Life, and this life brought light to mankind. The light shines in the darkness, and the darkness has never put it out." (John1: 4-5).
       He has come to save his people.
       He has come to redeem, to buy back.
       He has come to save us from the *Slavery of Sin*.
       He has come to establish his *Father's Kingdom on Earth*. God sent Jesus, his only Son, with 'The New Covenant'.

V4   If re-creation is going to come out of chaos then something has to change and that is, the rebellion of man. Therefore repentance has to be preached. This means that man must turn away from the darkness of *Satan*, and walk in the light with Jesus, *Keeping God's Laws*. The Kingdom of God has come and conversion is therefore essential if man is to save himself. Satan can only rule in a person or place where he is allowed!

V5   Many people prepare themselves for the coming of the Kingdom of God. "They confessed their sins and he baptised them in the River Jordan."

Baptism means to be immersed in the power of God, to be filled with the gift of Grace; to die to the old life of sin and accept a new life with the Messiah. This gift of Grace is an acceptance into God's Family, his love, friendship and everlasting union with him in the New Covenant.

V6   John the Baptist is the Son of the Priest, Zacharias, and Elizabeth. It is written in St. Luke's Gospel that he will be great in the eyes of God for he will bring many people of Israel back to the Lord. (Luke 1: 76-80). John is a very holy man and from an early age of his manhood he lives and wanders in the deserts around the Dead Sea. It is through John's great insight into the holy law of God that he spent thirty years of his life praying, fasting and preaching about the coming of the Messiah. John hates evil and when at times he does come out of the desert, men who are sinners become more tolerant with their neighbours, while others go and hide for they fear John.

V7   Here John humbly announces the expectation of the man who is to come. Someone who is exceptionally great. So great, that John states he would be totally unworthy of even kneeling down to "untie his sandals."

V8   He clearly distinguishes his Baptism with water with the fact that the 'one who will come' will Baptise them with the Holy Spirit. This fulfils the prophecy from the Old Testament when the Lord says to Moses; "I will send them a Prophet like you from among their own people. I will tell him what to say and he will tell the people everything I command. He will speak in my name, and I will punish anyone who refuses to obey him." (Deuteronomy 18: 18-19.)

So Jesus will come as his Father's representative and in his Father's name establish the Kingdom of God on earth.

Man cannot build the Kingdom of God for God in their own power because they are not up against men. Man is up against the power of *Evil, Wickedness,* and *Sinfulness of Man.*

Therefore Man has to be filled with God's power. We have got to have God's *Armour* on, (*Sacrament of Confirmation*), and use God's weapons because it is a *Spiritual Warfare.* "The

weapons we use in our fight are not the world's weapons but God's powerful weapons which we use to destroy evil." (2 Corinthians 10: 4.)

Through the Gospels we have to learn what the strongholds of *Satan* are that we have to pull down in the world in the name of God. So to do his will we need the *Power* of God, the Baptism of the Holy Spirit.

The Baptism and Temptation of Jesus

V9   Even though Jesus does not need to repent, for he had committed no sin, he asks John to Baptise him for he knows it is God's will. It also fulfils the teachings of John and shows the people that he is one of them. Indeed, is it here that Jesus realises that this is to be his first step towards Calvary, which is to be the whole aim of his life. Certainly the moment Jesus moves towards his Baptism, he is now being proclaimed the new Moses about to lead the new Exodus, of a new people, to a promised land. Moses led the people out of physical slavery in Egypt through the waters of the Red Sea, through the wilderness into the promised land. Jesus is now going to lead us out of the 'Slavery of Sin', through the waters of *Baptism*, through the wilderness to our promised land. So now you have:-

a)   The New Law – God's Law, A Law of Love.
b)   The New Creation – Conversion – A new life.
c)   The Redemption – Salvation made possible for man.

V10   As Jesus came out of the water 'he saw heaven opening, and the Spirit coming down on him like a dove.'

When Jesus dies you are going to have the veil of the temple torn apart from top to bottom, signifying the death of Judaism. The people in the Old Testament cry out to God "Why don't you tear the sky apart and come down . . ." (Isaiah 64: 1). We are seeing here the fulfilment of many texts from the Old Testament.

The Gospel of John records that it will be a sign that John the Baptist will recognise that this person is the Messiah: — "And

I tell you that he is the Son of God" (John 1: 34). "There is the lamb of God" (John 1: 36). The dove, symbolic of the Spirit of his Father entering into him, helps us to perceive the kind of *Messiah* that he will be. We associate the *Dove* as a sign of **Peace**.

V11 Jesus hears the *Voice* of his Father. This fulfils the prophecy in (Isaiah 42: 1). The Lord says, "Here is my servant, whom I strengthen—the one I have chosen, with whom I am pleased. I have filled him with my spirit...". Thus we have here the declaration that Jesus is God's representative, a servant ready and willing to do the work of his Father. He is the one through whom God's perfect work of Redemption will be accomplished.

V12 Whether you are a King or servant, there is always a time of testing. Here Jesus goes out into the wilderness to be tested. Every child of God has to be tested to see what is inside of him.

V13 Jesus is in the desert for 40 days. It is interesting to note that in Scripture the Number 40 has a deep symbolic meaning. Whenever the Number 40 turns up, usually the person or people are being prepared for a deeper revelation of God or for a deep decision in God's service.

Jesus comes out from being tested having made a clear decision, and he is fully aware of what God is asking of him. In the following Old Testament reading we can see how and why Moses and his people were tested.

"Remember how the hand of God led you on this long journey through the desert these past 40 years, sending hardship to test you, so that he might know what you intended to do and whether you would obey his commands. He made you go hungry, and then he gave you manna to eat, food that you and your ancestors had never eaten before. He did this to teach you that man must not depend on bread alone to sustain him, but on everything that the Lord says. During these 40 years your clothes have not worn out, nor have your feet swollen up.

Remember that the Lord your God corrects and punishes you just as a father disciplines his children. So then, do as the Lord has commanded you; live according to his Laws and obey

him." (Deuteronomy 8: 2-6).

God has to allow difficult situations to come our way. Many problems and disasters will come into our lives. In other words, we too will be tried and tested to see what we are made of. When someone hurts you, makes you angry or uncharitable, God is showing you what is deep inside your heart. You must hand it over to him and he will heal you:- (Reconciliation).

God will never desert us and through all our trials and troubles on this earth he is training us for the one true prize, *The Kingdom of God*. We make the choice, for we cannot serve *Two Masters*!

It is better to be tried and tested and proved as gold, then God can use us as his instruments in the world. The gifts of the Holy Spirit are only safe in the hands of a *Servant* and *Jesus* is portrayed as a *Servant* in Mark's Gospel. God can put the most important work ever to be done into the hands of Jesus because he is God's holy servant. He is meek and lowly of heart. When When Satan tempts or tries Jesus he fails continually; he finds no sin in Jesus—the only time he finds a man of 'Pure Gold'.

Jesus Calls Four Fishermen

V14   John stays in his own area preaching until he is arrested by Herod's soldiers.

Jesus goes to Galilee in Northern Israel. It is the home area of Jesus. Some of his disciples also come from this area, but it is here that he starts his Public Ministry; to found the Kingdom of His Father.

V15   "The Kingdom of God" is the reign of God in each one of our hearts. We have the responsibility to turn away from sin and let God enter our hearts. We must allow his rule to take over and this is how we co-operate to bring the Kingdom of God on Earth. As each person does this then we become a community.

V16   As Jesus walks along the side of Lake Galilee he sees his first two disciples. Being a wise servant he chooses helpers and delegates authority to them

V17   He calls to them. "I will teach you". This means that if Jesus calls you he will give you the grace and ability to carry out the work he has called you to do.

V18   Jesus offers Simon and his brother, Andrew, this great challenge to save men. They accept, and follow him.

V19   Jesus sees James and his brother, John, later to be nicknamed "Sons of Thunder," because when people refused to be converted they want to bring down fire and brimstone from Heaven.

V20   Jesus calls James and John and they also leave their work and follow him.

No doubt they were in great awe of him and recognised his authority.

A Man with An Evil Spirit

V21   Capernaum is to the North-West shore of Lake Galilee and it is here that Jesus spends most of his time while preaching in Galilee. It is interesting to note that throughout the Scriptures, whenever Jesus meets people who are in need, or making mistakes, or lost, he spends time teaching them. This is a major part of his work and then he will go away and pray to His Father.

On the Sabbath, we find Jesus preaching in the 'Synagogue' a Greek word meaning 'bringing together'.

Jewish custom allows the ruler of the Synagogue to invite any well known person to preach!

V22   Jesus preaches in the Synagogue and, unlike the Scribes, he makes a most profound impression on the people. They "are amazed" with his words of *Authority* 'I Say To You'.

They are moved by what they hear because *His Words* carry a mighty message and are filled with the *Power of God.*

V23   They are to be further *Amazed* when they are to become witnesses to *Real Power, God's Authority Over Evil.*

Here Jesus faces the power of *Darkness, Evil,* in a person.

V24   The unclean spirit shouts "Are you here to destroy us? I know who you are, you are God's holy messenger!" It is the unclean spirit in the man shouting, not the man. It is Satan himself, and he knows it is Jesus for they have met before.

Notice that spirits easily recognise God and yet people can be so utterly blind.

V25   The word of *Authority* comes sharply from Jesus, "Be quiet and come out of the man!" Wherever Jesus comes Satan loses ground and we see this all the time in the Scriptures.

V26   The man is healed, the evil spirit leaves him by *God's Authority.*

V27   The people are left amazed by what they have heard and seen. They recognise that Jesus' has authority over evil.

V28   The power over darkness, the light and love of God for his people makes its presence. For this is the beginning of his reputation which will spread throughout Galilee.

Jesus Heals Many People

V29   They take Jesus "straight away" to the home of Simon and Andrew, in other words, immediately. These are words that you would associate with a *Servant.* Thus you have Jesus doing the work of his Father and fulfilling his Father's will with instant obedience.

V30   Here we learn that Simon Peter is a married man and Jesus is told of the mother-in-law's sickness.

V31   He 'took her by the hand', and with quiet *Authority* he commands the sickness to leave her. She is cured. These words could also reflect the eye-witness account of Peter.

V32   Here we see his *Authority* continuing to heal and cure the people who come to him.

V33   The works and teaching of Jesus have spread so quickly that the whole town have come to him.

We need to remember that when God heals us, no matter what our sickness is, he wants us in return to *Serve His Church, His People and to walk in His Footsteps.*

V34   Look at the word "*Many*" because it is very important! Why did Jesus not cure *All* the people? Can you cure a person that does not want to be cured? The biggest block in a person receiving Jesus into their lives is their unbelief!

You also have a reference to what the scholars call the *Messianic* Secret, that is where, in the Gospel of Mark, Jesus plays down his role as the *Messiah.* The reason for this is because

the people are expecting a *Political Figure*. They are expecting a *Messiah* who will overthrow the *Romans* and make *Israel*
the greatest nation on *Earth*. But what about the rest of the
world? When Jesus is in the wilderness he chooses to fulfil the
prophecies of *Isaiah* which tells us about the humble, suffering
Servant who will lay down his life for all mankind. We can also
read that he fulfilled the prophecy in (Philippians 2: 6-11).

"He always had the nature of God but he did not think that by
force he should try to become equal with God. Instead of this,
of his own free will he gave up all he had, and took the nature of a Servant. He became like man and appeared in human
likeness. He was humble, and walked the path of obedience all
the way to his death–on a cross. For this reason God raised
him to the highest place above and gave him the name that is
greater than any other name.

And so, in honour of the name of Jesus, all beings in heaven,
on earth and in the world below will fall on their knees and all
will openly proclaim that Jesus Christ is Lord, to the Glory of
God the Father."

So Jesus plays everything down until the *Passion* and *Resurrection* when you see Jesus as the *Messiah*.

Jesus Preaches in Galilee

V35   Jesus must have been exhausted, yet he gets up and goes to
find a quiet place where he speaks with his Father. No doubt
he was seeking his Father's guidance and we notice that this
occurs on many occasions in the Scriptures.

V36   The disciples go in search of Jesus.

V37   They tell him that the people are looking for him.

V38   Jesus tells his disciples where they must go next.
Here, travelling through Galilee he teaches and heals. He is in
fact doing his Father's will.

Jesus Heals a Man

V40   Leprosy is a terrible and loathsome disease, but very common
in these days. A leper is isolated, as there is no cure and they

are not allowed to mix among the people, or come into the city. Not only are they considered unclean in body, but for the Jews it is a symbol of a great sin that has been committed. Note that if you leave sin unchecked in a person's life it will gradually eat away at the character of the person and he will become completely rotten *Spiritually.*

Obviously this man has heard of Jesus, and has found a way to see him. The Leper knows Jesus can cure him but is he truly willing?

V41 Jesus touches the man. According to the Law of Moses, if you touch a Leper, it makes you unclean and you will have to go through the rites of cleansing which can last up to seven days.

V42 The man is now clean and transformed. Jesus wants to touch and transform us in our lives, but are we willing?

V43 Jesus "spoke sternly to him"; is this because Jesus knows that there is some doubt or weakness in the man's character?

V44 Throughout the Scriptures the Scribes and the Pharisees accuse Jesus of breaking the Law of Moses. However he only breaks the parts of the Law that are interpreted in a certain way, whereby the people obey *Laws* but not always the *Law of God.* It is not against the Law of Moses to make a person whole again. Technically, Jesus may have been touching an unclean person, but the moment Jesus touches him that person is no longer unclean; so he is not breaking the Law.

Jesus asks the man not to tell people about the cure, but to present himself to the Priests. Here we see Jesus recognising the normal authority and you will find him recognising it in Church and State.

He says in his teachings that he has not come to destroy the Law of Moses, but rather to see that it is fulfilled,

"Offer the sacrifice that Moses ordered."

V45 The man goes away and does the opposite to what Jesus has asked of him. He does not remain quiet but tells everyone about his cure. Is this the weakness in the man, his disobedience rather than gratitude? Jesus wants him to keep silent because the Jews have the wrong image of the *Messiah* and Jesus wants them to learn the true and correct image, but this is going to take time. Jesus pays a price for healing this disobedient man by leaving the town and living in the open.

Questions Mark Chapter One

1. Why does Mark not mention the genealogy of Jesus?
2. What does the word 'Messiah' mean?
3. What does the word 'Covenant' mean?
4. Why does God send Jesus onto this earth?
5. What do you understand by the word 'Baptism'?
6. Why do we need to be Baptised?
7. Who is the 'Messenger'? Give two reasons why he is an important figure in the Gospel story.
8. Why does Jesus ask to be Baptised and who does the voice from heaven say he is?
9. What does the dove symbolise?
10. Which Prophet tells us that God wanted Jesus to be His Servant on this earth?
11. Why is Jesus tempted?
12. Why does God test us?
13. Where does Jesus start his Public Ministry?
14. Why does Jesus choose disciples?
15. What is the name of the place where Jesus spends most of his time, when in Galilee?
16. What does the Greek word 'Synagogue' mean?
17. What do the people find 'amazing' about Jesus?
18. Who are the ones who recognise Jesus?
19. Why does Jesus not cure all the people?
20. What reference do you find to the *Messianic Secret*? Explain why he plays down his role as the Messiah.
21. Why does Jesus tell the Leper to keep quiet and to present himself before the Priests?
22. Why do you think Jesus spoke sternly to him?

St. Mark Chapter Two

Jesus Heals A Paralysed Man

In the Scriptures we notice that Jesus always accomplishes his good works wherever there is *Faith*. *Faith* is believing and *Trusting* in *God's Word, His Love, His Mercy* and *His Power*. However, *if there is no Faith,* Jesus is not free to do his work.

This is still true to-day. If we close our hearts to *Faith*, if we hold doubts about the *Existence* of Jesus, his power to transform; then he will never be able to enter our hearts. Here we have an excellent example of *Faith!*

V1   After living in the 'open' Jesus returns to his home. Nazareth is his real home, so we presume that this must have been Peter's house in Capernaum.

V2   When people hear, they gather in their hundreds, as there appears to be no room, not only in the house, but also around it.

V3   Four men with great *Faith* arrive with their friend who is sick.

V4   We realise the greatness of their *Faith* because they are so determined to get their friend to Jesus that they make "an opening" in the roof and lower him down 'on his mat' into the house. Here Jesus accomplishes two points.

a) He responds to the *Faith* of these men and their sick friend.

b) He uses this situation to get his teaching over to the people who are all around him. Jesus knows that many of these people are in greater need than the Paralytic, because he has faith and is ready to change his life. However, many of the people around him are not ready to repent and change their lives. Therefore, under these circumstances, he hopes to get through to the hearts of those standing around him!

It is here that we see the first step of *Opposition* to *Jesus*.

V5   Jesus sees that the paralysis in this man is nothing! The most important concern that Jesus has for this man is the sin in his life and his unrepentant heart. That is why he tells him that he can be free of his sin, which is his major problem! So this man receives a most fantastic gift, his sins are forgiven and he is filled with God's Grace.
This is true of us to-day. God gave us this 'fantastic Gift' of *Reconciliation* but how many take it seriously? *Sin* destroys the soul of man and makes him rotten inside, unfit for the Kingdom of God. Jesus wants us all to be free of sin, to be beautiful inside, to be filled with God's Grace and fit to live with His Father one day in *Heaven*!

V6   Here we see people sitting around who think they have no problems and no sin in their hearts. Yet they are going to sit in judgement on Jesus, the Son of God. That can also be our problem too. We sometimes sit in judgement on our neighbours and this is a very serious block between us and God.

V7   Here we see the Jews taking their first stand in *Opposition* to Jesus and they accuse him of 'Blaspheming'. Why? This is due to the fact that they are taught in the Old Testament that only God can forgive *Sin*. However Jesus does not say "I am God", he only says "My son, your sins are forgiven."

V8   Jesus can read their minds and thoughts just as he can with us! He knows exactly what is going through their minds. If he is genuinely capable of forgiving sin, then he must be God.

V9   So Jesus answers their problem, and shows them that he has divine *Authority* when he states that it is no more difficult to say "Your sins are forgiven" or to say "Get up, pick up your mat and walk."

V10   Here we see Jesus teaching about *Authority* This is the first time in the Gospel that he refers to himself as 'The Son of Man'.

V11   Jesus is showing them that there is *Divine Authority* in his words. This is also the only miracle in relation to *Forgiveness*.

V12   The people are amazed because they had never experienced anything like this before. Obviously they have seen that Jesus did have the power to forgive sin. Even so, there are still those in the crowd who will continue to oppose the teachings of Jesus because their hearts are so stubborn.

Jesus Calls Levi

V13 Jesus returns to Lake Galilee and continues his teachings as he walks along the shore.

V14 Jesus sees 'a tax collector, Levi Son of Alphaeus', later to be known as Matthew. Jesus calls him to be a disciple and Levi obeys Jesus and leaves his very prosperous business of being a tax collector. Levi is known to be a hard-headed business man. What is it that makes him decide to give his wealth up and follow Jesus? Is it that he has the insight to see that earthly wealth is only short term and that Heavenly wealth will never end?

V15 Levi invites Jesus to a meal. Many of Levi's friends who are tax-collectors and other sinners also come. We see through the Scriptures that many of these people come into the Kingdom of God far more quickly than those who think that they are religious!

V16 In the eyes of the Pharisees Jesus is for the second time breaking the Law of Moses.

To the Jew, tax collectors or Roman word "Publicani" are to be despised and considered as outcasts because they work for the Romans collecting the taxes. Sinners are people who do not keep to the strict Law of Moses and please themselves how they live. Thus they are considered unclean and here is Jesus eating and mixing with these people. To sit and have a meal is a sign of friendship.

V17 Jesus hears what they are saying about him and he asks them if they are sick? He tells them that he has only come for the sick and those who are in need; and if they are not in need they do not belong to his Kingdom. We have already learnt that the first step to enter God's Kingdom is *Repentance*. Therefore the first thing I have to admit is that I am a sinner, so I need God, I need a Saviour and I am prepared to let him into my heart. But Jesus is addressing people who consider that they are living 'a perfect life'. They keep the Laws of Moses, fast twice a week and pay their taxes. However, Jesus is trying to get over to them that he is not interested in what they do because that will not save them. It is their hearts that need to change and this is what Jesus is after.

So we see here Jesus challenging Pharisees to admit that they are sinners so that they can come into the Kingdom and be saved.

The Question about Fasting

Now you will see that the Scribes and Pharisees are always following him around and forever criticising him

V18   At this time John the Baptist is in prison and it seems very reasonable that his followers, who love him dearly, will want to fast in sadness for the situation which he is in.

V19   Here Jesus explains to the people, that while he is on earth, he wants his disciples to rejoice in his company. Jesus is a very human person and so ordinary that they cannot believe he is God. Although they have seen his works, the power of his word and know that his power is greater than any man's they have ever met, they still cannot believe.

He likens the situation to that of a Wedding. He is the Bridegroom, of the *New Israel* and his disciples are his representatives. Therefore, whilst he is with them, they should rejoice and feast.

V20   For when the Bridegroom goes, which is a reference to the Death Jesus will have to face, the disciples will no longer feast but fast for their Saviour. You see the great love Jesus has for his Church. Right from the beginning he will call his Church his Bride and Himself, the Bridegroom.

V21   He is saying here that *Judaism* is so old and so far gone, that you cannot patch it up anymore, it is *Finished!*

When Jesus dies, the veil of the temple before the Holy of Holies, which symbolises the most sacred thing in *Judaism*, is torn from top to bottom, thus symbolising the death of *Judaism.*

V22   Jesus is saying here that the old covenant (old wine skins) has gone and it is finished. God has sent him to replace it with a new covenant, a new arrangement between God and man. (New wine poured into new wineskins). Jesus tells them that the Gospel of grace cannot mix with the legalism of the Jewish religion, they will destroy each other. *Grace* is a free gift that we first receive in our Baptism and we become a child of God;

and he becomes our Loving Father. It is a relationship that grows through our lives.

Here Jesus is saying 'You shall love God with your whole heart, your whole soul, your whole mind, and your whole being, and then you shall love your neighbour as you love yourself'.

The legalism of the Jews is far too rigid. You can barely move or breathe for their Laws and *Love* is certainly lacking!

They have 613 rules for the Sabbath day alone.

Jesus has not come to burden his people but to open up for them 'Freedom', the essence of which is the Law of Love.

He comes to set them free and to give them the Holy Spirit of God, which is the mark of Joy. Jesus cannot pour new wine, the *New Covenant*, on to their legalism. The Scribes and Pharisees resent being told that they are wrong. They resent any form of change to the *Old Law*.

The Question about the Sabbath

V23   Would you like people talking about everything you said or did? In other words 'always being on your back!' Well, that is the situation for Jesus and his disciples. The Scribes and Pharisees are always watching and listening closely to their conversation. Have you ever plucked at long grass as you walked through a field? I know I have. The disciples here do something similar.

V24   However they are to be accused of breaking the 'Sabbath Law'. It is forbidden to reap your harvest on the Sabbath Day. This is to pick the ears of corn and grind it down.

Therefore if they want to eat it, they will have to grind it with their hands and for this they are accused of harvesting and threshing on the Sabbath. Can you see now what has happened to *Judaism*? They have gone so Legalistic that they have taken their Laws to the extreme. There is no freedom at all, but Jesus defends them and goes on to tell them that God wants his people free!

V25   Jesus asks them if they have ever read what David did in a time of need. (1 Samuel 21: 1-6). David is fleeing from King

Saul and he and his men are very hungry, as they have run out of supplies.

V26   David goes to the High Priest, Ahimelech, as he has no ordinary bread he gives them the the Sacred bread to eat. Jesus is saying here that he is not doing something new because the Jews always make reference to Moses or David; and yet David was not accused of 'breaking the Law'. Jesus is trying to explain to them that David understood God's Law. David understood that under normal circumstances the Sacred bread would only be eaten by the Priests, but David was God's anointed King. Therefore, he could make the decision that in this situation of great need and grave danger, they could eat the bread and God would not consider it to be a sin.

V27   Here Jesus is saying that man must not be put into slavery; he wants man free. God made the Sabbath for man to rest. Thus man will then be more healthy, both physically and spiritually, and he will also have time to worship the Lord. The Sabbath is made for our good, that we will give him one day out of seven!

Jesus here is claiming to be greater than the Law of Moses. Still at this stage Jesus cannot openly claim to be the *Messiah*. He knows what is in their hearts. He knows that they expect a *Messiah* who will come in Great Glory and Splendour with an army to destroy the Romans. They cannot accept this humble servant and the whole of Mark's Gospel is to show mankind that Jesus chose to be God's Holy Servant.

V28   Capital S, Capital M = Son of Man. It is the title for the *Messiah*.

"I saw what looked like a human being; Son of Man. He was approaching me, surrounded by clouds, and he went to the one who had been living forever and was presented to him. He was given authority, honour and royal power, so that the people of all nations, races and languages would serve him. This authority would last forever, and his Kingdom would never end." (Daniel 7: 13-14).

Thus we have *Son of God, Son of Man*. Jesus is very gently, and with tremendous discretion, feeding his people with the knowledge that he is the *Messiah, but the people are still not ready within their hearts and minds to grasp the wisdom of his words and works. Jesus is fully aware of the situation and this is why he treats his claim to being the Messiah with such delicacy.*

Questions Mark Chapter Two

1. What does Jesus see in the four men who bring their sick friend to him?
2. How does Jesus use this situation?
3. What is Jesus concerned about in this man?
4. What is the reaction of the teachers of the Law?
5. How does Jesus react to their problem?
6. Why do you think Levi followed Jesus?
7. Why is Jesus accused of breaking the Law?
8. What lesson does Jesus try to get over to them when he knows they are criticising him?
9. How does Jesus answer their question on fasting?
10. What is Jesus telling us when he refers to old and new wineskins?'
11. How does Jesus answer them concerning the question about the Sabbath?

St. Mark Chapter Three

The Man with a Paralysed Hand

V1   Jesus goes back to His Father's House to be with his people who are in need. Here he finds a man in need of healing.

V2   Now we are going to step into further dispute over the Laws of the Sabbath.

People are there who are aware that this man needed healing, but the real reason for their presence is to collect evidence against Jesus! So it will be reasonable to say that they clearly have 'premeditated murder' in their hearts already.

V3   Jesus tells the man to come to the front. Notice Jesus does not touch him.

V4   The Law of Moses allows only serious cases of illness to be treated on the Sabbath Day. However Jesus is asking them here which is right, to do good or evil? They cannot say 'evil', so they say nothing; which makes them look very foolish! This adds to their hate and jealousy of Jesus.

V5   Jesus is angry because of their obstinacy and sad because they are blocking their hearts to the words of God.

Jesus heals the man by word. Therefore the Scribes and Pharisees cannot accuse Jesus of breaking the Law of the Sabbath.

V6   The Pharisees then gather together with some Herodians; they are a mixture of both political and religious people. Their intention of 'premeditated murder' is finally formed and they plan to kill Jesus. It is interesting, though sad, to note that they do not consider their action of planning to kill Jesus as a **sin**!

It is no wonder that Jesus once referred to them 'as white washed tombs'. In other words you can look beautiful on the outside but inside, like the dead bodies, you are rotten.

The Jewish way of love is to fulfil all the external Laws. If they are to change their hearts and this is what Jesus wants, then the whole of society and even the world, will have to change. Jesus does speak to them about this in detail in 'The Sermon on the Mount'. (Matthew 5).

A Crowd by the Lake

V7   Jesus leaves Capernaum and goes with his disciples to the shores of Lake Galilee. However large numbers of people follow him.

V8   Even more crowds gather. The popularity of Jesus and his works have spread far and wide.

V9   The crowds are so numerous that Jesus has to get a boat to preach from, otherwise he will be crushed.

V10   All the ordinary, simple people who follow him think he is wonderful. Many obviously recognise the presence of God and are in great need of healing. Do these people want to repent or have they come just to be healed? It appears that all they want is to touch him in order to be healed. They do not seem to want to repent, so is this pure selfishness within their hearts? Or is the block one of blindness? Is this not true of Christians to-day? We want to be physically healed of our illnesses, but are we prepared to follow and fulfil the word of God in our every day lives and to be spiritually healed? Are our hearts loving and kind or do we allow Satan to enter and put jealousy or hate there instead?

V11   Again it is interesting to see that *Evil* always recognises *God*. They know that Jesus is the the *Master* over evil. They throw themselves down before him and worship him. As Christians, how much time do we give to repent and do God's work among our neighbours?

V12   He orders them to keep quiet for he wants to continue his lowly role of God's Servant on earth. He has His Father's mission to complete and already the Pharisees and Scribes are planning to kill him.

Jesus Chooses the Twelve Apostles

V13   Here Jesus chooses 'the men he wanted'. He obviously knows the kind of people they are and that they will fulfil what he knows has to be fulfilled.

V14   The number 12 represents the twelve tribes of Old Israel, but these twelve Apostles which means 'sent', are going to be God's representatives in the 'New Israel'. Notice the first duty Jesus gives them. It is to be his companions, his friends! Does this not show us how human Jesus is? He is then going to teach them, so that they will be able to teach others.

V15   He also promises to give them *Authority* to cast out evil spirits. He is in fact preparing them to be God's representatives in building up the Christian Church.

V16   Here follow the names of the Apostles he chooses. They are ordinary men but obviously their personalities are different.
For example, Peter always seems to get into a 'spot of bother' and Jesus has to 'put him in order' on occasions. However Jesus makes Peter the leader because he knows that he has a 'big heart'. He has the gift of love!

V17   James and John are 'fiery young men' perhaps that is why Jesus calls them 'Boanerges', which means 'Men of Thunder'.

V18   Here we have the names of the rest of his *Apostles*. It is interesting to note the differences in the men. Apart from what is mentioned earlier, we have Levi or Matthew who is a tax collector and considered a traitor to his people. Simon, James and John are upper class for they are owners of trawlers and Simon is also a Zealot. Zealots are like a resistance movement fighting to defeat the Roman Army in their country. Already we have two men, Matthew the traitor and Simon the Zealot, in opposition to each other's way of life.

V19   Then there is Judas, who is certainly commissioned by Jesus, but we do get inklings of him slowly falling as we go through the Gospels. Judas loved money and in fact he is given the job of looking after the finances of the Apostles.
Is this truly his weakness and is the time of his 'calling' to the time of him 'falling' not a lesson for us?
However, in spite of their differences, they have one thing in common and that is their Great Love for Jesus. It kept them

totally united as a community. Christians to-day can only be a community when they are in union with the Love of God and their neighbour! Are you?

Jesus and Beelzebul

V20 When he returns to Capernaum Jesus is met by such a huge crowd of people in need that there is not even time to get something to eat. He is putting his neighbour before himself, yet another example for us!

V21 The great demands of his work must have made him completely exhausted. People said, "He's gone mad", no doubt referring to the fact that he was working far too hard. However we all know how stories get out of context and his family hear the story that he has 'gone mad'. You can just imagine how Mary must have felt and what suffering she must have gone through. Yet she carries her cross with tremendous *Faith*, hearing exaggerated stories, lies, accusations right up to the death of Her Beloved Son.
So I think that it is very important to remember that even the *Mother of God* is tried, but finally becomes *Queen of Heaven*. His family come to see what is happening.

V22 Some of the Pharisees begin to accuse him of being devil-possessed. In other words being full of Satan!

V23 Jesus asks them if it is reasonable that Satan would cast Satan out of himself? Obviously not, you cannot cast yourself out of yourself. He explains to them that he cannot possibly work his exorcisms by the power of Satan. It is by the power of God that Satan is cast out and it means that God is present, he is here among you! Jesus continues to speak in *Parables*.

V24 If a country becomes divided it will result in a downfall.

V25 If families allow anger, jealousy, or hatred into their hearts, they will destroy themselves.

V26 Thus when Satan's Kingdom is divided it too will fall apart and be destroyed.

V27 Jesus here explains why he has come. 'A strong man's house' is the evil and wickedness of Satan on this earth. But Jesus 'ties up the strong man' when he performs his *Exorcisms*. God and Satan are to be found in people. We as individuals make the decision as to who will rule our lives, God or Satan!

God wants us all for his Kingdom where there is Eternal Happiness.

Satan, because he will never enter Heaven, wants us for Hell, where, like him, we would live in utter misery. It is our free choice and Jesus is telling the people and us that he has come to set the world free. His mission is to be *Our Saviour.*

V28   Repentance is within everyone's reach. Sins will be forgiven.

V29   There is only one unforgivable sin which can never be undone. That **sin** is to accuse God of being possessed by Satan. It is the worst possible form of blasphemy.

V30   Notice that the Jews are saying this about Jesus.

Jesus' Mother and Brothers

V31   The family of Jesus arrive and ask for him.

V32   The people tell him that his mother, brothers and sisters are waiting for him.

V33   Jesus asks "Who is my mother? Who are my brothers?"

V34-35 Here Jesus is saying that the lady outside who they call his mother, became his mother by doing the will of the Father. Therefore, those who desire to mother the church, to be his sister or brother, must also do the will of the Father.

Throughout Scripture Jesus tells us that it is no use just believing the word of God, we must put it into practice.

Questions Mark Chapter Three

1. Why are there further disputes over the Law of the Sabbath?
2. How does Jesus deal with this situation?
3. What does 'white washed tombs' mean in this situation?
4. What is the first order Jesus gave his Apostles?
5. Who are the twelve Apostles, and what do you know about them?
6. What is the great thing they had in common?
7. What do the Pharisees accuse Jesus of?
8. How does Jesus answer them?
9. What is the unforgivable sin?
10. When told that his mother and brothers are waiting for him, what lesson does Jesus give to the people?
11. What do you understand by Exorcism?

St. Mark Chapter Four

The Parable of the Sower: This is also an Allegory

V1   The crowds are so huge that they are spread along the shore and Jesus speaks to them from a boat out in the water.

V2   He speaks to them in *Parables*.

V3   This illustrates the work of Jesus in the world. Jesus preaches 'The word of God', which is the seed, to everyone no matter what spiritual condition they are in, and the *Soil* represents the people.
       Here Jesus tells us that there are four kinds of *Soil* (people). Biologically you can change one kind of *Soil* into another. Therefore man can change from doing *Evil* to doing *Good*, doing the will of God!

V4   These people are indifferent to the word of God, they have *No Faith*.

V5-6   These people start off well, but give up when things do not go their way or life becomes hard. They show little Faith in the word of God.

V7   These people are keen when they start but as time goes on, other desires, interests, bad companions destroy the Faith in their lives. They show little Faith in the word of God.

V8   These people grow in harmony with the word of God which shows great Faith.
       Here we see that the growth of their Faith varies for some bear more fruit than others. Faith is a slow, spiritual process of believing, trusting, accepting, forgiving and loving God as Our Father and Our Saviour. However, some people grow spiritually more quickly than others, for example 'the Saints'. I think we should ask ourselves what kind of soil am I? Do I bear *Fruit*? What is *Fruit*? "*Love, Joy, Peace,*

Patience, Kindness, Goodness, Faithfulness, Humility, and Self-control." (Galatians 5: 22). Jesus is telling the people that the word of God will bear *Fruit*. "So also will be the word I speak–it will not fail to do what I plan for it, it will do everything I send it to do." (Isaiah 55: 11).

V9   Jesus is asking them to open up their hearts to the word of God.

The Purpose of the Parables

V10   They ask for the *Parables* to be explained to them.
V11   Here Jesus divides the people into those that believe and those that refuse to hear the word of God. To his disciples and others that believe, Jesus tells them that he has given the parable that they might understand and he will explain everything to them. The disciples alone already know the meaning of the 'Secret'; that is the truth about God's Kingdom.
The man on the outside is the worldly man, who has no knowledge of God and no Faith.
Jesus says that if you try to get through to him and tell him about spiritual things even through a Parable, they will not understand you. There are some who will never respond to God's word!
V12   They see physically, but spiritually they are blind. They hear physically, but spiritually they are deaf to the word of God. Their hearts are hard and they refuse to change and become converted.
This does not mean that people who are without *Faith* cannot ever become converted. It means that those of us who do believe must pray for our neighbours that God will open their eyes, ears and hearts to the word of God. God said "I will look for those that are lost, bring back those that wander off." (Ezekiel 34: 16).

Jesus Explains the Parable of the Sower

V13   Is Jesus here telling us that to understand the word of God we must be in close union with him? Even though we believe we

must pray that God will continue to 'open our eyes, ears and hearts' even more! Conversion is something that will go on all through our lives because it is a life long process!

V14   Jesus preaches the word of God.

V15   'Some people', that is us, allow Satan to destroy the word of God within us very quickly.

V16-17 When persecution comes they fall away. For example people at work may pass remarks like 'he's gone religious', 'he goes to Mass', 'he actually says prayers'. There are people who just cannot take this and so they give up and go along with the crowd, so as not to be the odd one out. How sad, see how much they need our prayers!

V18-19 God will give us anything that he knows will be good for us. Here people become materialistic and full of all the worries and fears of this world. Thus the word of God does not take root in the soul, it is choked by greed and all the materialistic things of this life. This is the rule of Satan. God's rule is for you to be at peace and full of joy. Who is ruling your life?

V20   There are people who have given their lives to God, live a life of prayer and genuinely live up to the word of God. These are the people who will produce the harvest for the Lord.

A Lamp under a Bowl

V21   Lamp means 'the light of *Faith*'. Jesus is saying here that no-one should hide their *Faith*. During your life he gives you the opportunity to show him what is inside of you. If there is anything inside that comes out into his light that needs to be healed or transformed, he will heal you. (*Reconciliation*) Therefore let the light of *Faith* be seen by others in your life.

V22   Do not hide anything because one day it will have to come out. There will be the Day of Judgement. Therefore get rid of your sins now, anger, pride, unforgiveness for example. Then on the Day of Judgement you can stand before the Lord and your works will be pleasing to him.

V23   Jesus is asking them to let the word of God enter their hearts. This requires them to stop being deaf and to 'open their ears' *spiritually*.

The Measure

V24   Jesus says here that the amount of criticism, jealousy, un-forgiveness, hatred, uncharitableness, that you give out to people, is the amount that you will get back and more besides. However the amount of love, generosity, compassion that you give out is the amount that you will get back and more besides. *Disciples* are to be *Givers* not *Grabbers*!

V25   Notice the material things of this life decrease in value and become worn as they are used. Yet the more we use the Spiritual Gifts the more our *Faith* increases. Use 'little *Faith*' and it will grow, use the growth you have got, until you have great *Faith*. God has given us the Gift of Love, if we use it, our love will increase. It is the exact opposite to *Material* things! If you have *Faith* and you do not use it, it will grow smaller. If you continue not to use it, it will grow even smaller and you will be in *Danger* of losing it altogether!

We must use our *Spiritual Gifts*. We receive these in our *Confirmation*.

Wisdom – divine direction

Understanding – belief in our Christian Faith

Counsel – making the right Judgement

Fortitude – courage to fulfil our beliefs

Knowledge – living a charitable life

Piety – reverence for and respect for his children

The Fear of the Lord – Awe and love for God's Presence

The Parable of The Growing Seed

V26-29   Here is the Kingdom of God. The seed has been put into the world quietly with a *Divine Energy* that will prevent anyone from stopping its growth! Its growth will be slow and gradual. It will produce a harvest, but it will come in God's time, not in man's time. Jesus is saying that the Kingdom has already come and that when God enters your life you will grow slowly but positively if you let him take you over! People who are dedicated to the 'Word of God' will grow spiritually through

his power and those who do the 'Father's Will', will one day enter the Kingdom.

The Parable of the Mustard Seed

V30-32 Here Jesus speaks about the tiniest of seeds, the mustard seed which comes from the black mustard. This is a very thick bush that can also grow into a large tree and it grows wild in Israel. We can also read about a tree that will fill the whole earth:-
"Its leaves were beautiful and it had enough fruit on it to feed the whole world.
Wild animals rested under it, and birds made nests in its branches." (Daniel 4: 21).

Jesus is that Tree

He says I know you are very weak but my power is made perfect in your weakness. Open your hearts and let me work within you. Then I will let you become a tree that will fill the whole earth and 'the birds of the air' will nest in its branches. The 'birds of the air' is an uncomplimentary term used by many Rabbis when discussing the Gentiles. The parable also refers to the spread of the Christian Church.
"The wild animals bore their young in its shelter; The nations of the world rested in its shade." (Ezekiel 31: 6).
This means that the Kingdom of God is already casting its shadow for anyone who desires to shelter under it.
Jesus brings the 'Good News' which spreads quickly; is translated into all languages and now Christianity covers the whole world. No other man born has affected the human race as Jesus has. Why? Because he truly is *Our Saviour* and *Our King*.

V33 Why does he speak in *Parables*? So that they can go home and think about *His word.*

V34 Jesus is always ready to explain everything to his disciples. Their Faith is still a little weak but Jesus is going to show them in a very simple situation the greatness of His Power, which we find in V39.

Jesus Calms a Storm

V35   Jesus decides to go to the other side of the Lake.

V36   Jesus leaves the crowd behind him because they are in need of rest. Jesus must have been very tired after teaching in **Parables**.

V37   A sudden and strong storm starts to fill their boat.

V38   Jesus is asleep, which is a very normal thing to do when you are very tired. Notice the disciples seem only to have *Faith* in *Him* when he is awake. They are obviously frightened.

V39   Here he shows his disciples the greatness of His Power even over the elements. He reveals to them a supreme *Authority*! When he stands up, he speaks quietly. This miracle shows *Power* over nature.

V40   Jesus rebukes them about their *Faith*.

V41   There is a big difference in knowing Jesus of Nazareth, the man they walked with in Galilee and knowing Jesus the Christ. They are only gradually beginning to realise who he really is!

Questions Mark Chapter Four

1. Read the 'Parable of the Sower' and explain what it means.
2. Explain the meaning of 'A Lamp under a Bowl'.
3. What do you understand by the Parable of 'The Measure?'
4. How can we increase our Faith?
5. Read and explain the parable of the 'Mustard Seed'.
6. Give an account of a nature miracle.
7. Write a prayer or poem telling God that, with His Grace, you will be His instrument on this earth.
8. How can we best serve God in our lives?

St. Mark Chapter Five

Jesus Heals a Man with Evil Spirits

V1   Jesus and his disciples return to the other side of Lake Galilee where a steep cliff overhung the Lake. We know it is a place where wild pigs roam and there are many caves containing tombs.

V2   There is a man on the shore possessed by an unclean spirit.

V3   He lives in the tombs because he is also insane and the people can do nothing with him.

V4   The people have even tried to chain him down; this fails, because he is so completely under Satan's influence. Satan obviously has given him tremendous physical power.

V5   Notice the horrific effect when Satan is allowed to enter into a person's life. You find utter destruction of self!

V6   He runs up to Jesus and falls on his knees. It is Satan who is surrendering himself to Jesus not the man. Satan knows who Jesus is and this is before Calvary. Satan knows full well that he is doomed for eternity!

V7   Notice again how *Evil Spirits* recognise "Jesus, Son of the Most High God" long before *Man* does. It clearly shows man's blindness! Here Satan begs Jesus not to send him down to *Hell*. Satan knows that he is doomed for everlasting *Hell*, but that will come eventually in God's time.

V8   The unclean spirit did not move.

V9   Therefore Jesus asks him his name. Why? It is true that if you know a person's name you are that much closer to them and you have a certain amount of control over them.

It is interesting to note that God would not reveal his name when Moses begged him to. God replied to Moses "*I Am.*" The reason being that as sinners he must have known that

people would defile it. We only have to listen to the way many people use the word Jesus as a swear word, when in fact, they should bow their head when they hear the name of *Our Saviour*.

'Mob' or 'Legion' indicates that there are many evil spirits in the man. Legion is a division of three to six thousand Roman soldiers.

V10   Satan does not want to leave the place where he has achieved success. Always remember that Satan can only work in people when they allow him into their hearts.

This of course is *Satan's Aim*, to destroy man's salvation and take them to eternal *'Hell'* with him! We make the choice! Notice the number of times that the word begged is used.

V11   The pigs are near by.

V12   The Jews consider pigs to be very dirty animals and they are not allowed by the Law to eat or touch them. If they do touch them, they have to go to the Priest at the temple and be purified. This should help us to understand the situation, for here Jesus will get rid of unclean spirits and unclean animals at the same time.

V13   This is very interesting! Here you see that even the unclean pigs prefer *Death* rather than have unclean spirits in them. This is the only time Jesus cast out evil spirits into another place. Obviously both are destroyed when they drown. This should be a great lesson for all of us, because we see that the pigs resisted *Evil* and yet man will accept it!

V14   The news spreads and people come to see what is going on.

V15   The people have experienced two great miracles. The man who was insane is now sane. The evil is cast out and he is completely healed, both spiritually and physically.

The reaction of the people is fear. Why? Obviously they realise that Jesus is no ordinary man.

No ordinary man could have cured this 'mad man'. To perform this great miracle it is clear to the people that Jesus not only came from God, but has the *Power* of *God* within him.

V16   Those who have witnessed the miracle tell other people about what has happened.

V17   The reaction of the people is really beyond understanding for 'they asked Jesus to leave'. Why? Because Satan has made a

good home for himself in the hearts of many of those people who live there and they do not want to change. We realise this because Satan asks to be left there; he does not want to be sent away. Incredible when you think that Jesus is offering them *Redemption* but they turn it down! This is of course what we do when we refuse to listen to the word of God and just go our own way pleasing ourselves.

But at the end of our lives, from which none of us can escape, we will have to face the consequences of how we lived up to the *Word* of *God!*

V18   Here we see the man asking Jesus to let him serve him. He wants to go with Jesus.

V19   Jesus has work for this man but the work is there among his own people. Jesus tells the man to stay. He wants him to be a missionary in Satan's area. Jesus realises that these people need someone to help them and so he leaves this man to do this great work.

Notice the compassion Jesus has for them although they have rejected him. How would you react if someone rejected you?

V20   Have you noticed that on this occasion Jesus does not ask the man to keep quiet. In fact he has done the complete opposite. The man obeys the words of Jesus and goes away preaching to all the people in the ten towns, known as *Decapolis* and they listen to him.

"God purposely chose what the world considers nonsense in order to shame the wise, and he chose what the world considers weak in order to shame the powerful." (1: Corinthians 1: V27.)

Jairus' Daughter and the Woman Who Touched Jesus' Cloak

V21   Jesus and his disciples return across the Lake once more to be met by a large crowd, which means 'interruption', for they are demanding his attention. He is being interrupted from going for something to eat, to wash or even to rest for a while. How do you react to someone in your family, when you have been working hard and either you're watching television or preparing to go out and they ask you to do something for them? Do

	you sulk and refuse, or do you go and do the job with a smile on your face and love in your heart? There is only love in Jesus' heart!
V22	Jairus, a ruler of the local Synagogue comes and kneels at the feet of Jesus.
V23	Notice the word 'begs' appears once again. The man is in despair because his daughter is very sick. The 'laying on of hands' and receiving healing in this way was accepted in those days. The fact that he goes to Jesus, and not to a local Rabbi, plus begging Jesus to 'heal' her, indicates that this man has *Faith* in Jesus. As I said earlier, such is his love and compassion that he goes with Jairus.
V24	However they are interrupted on their journey due to narrow streets and the popularity of Jesus has become so great that the crowds press against him so that he can hardly move. You know that when famous people appear in public, like famous footballers, the Royal Family, or actors, they all have some form of protection from the public because people want to get near to touch them. Jesus just presses on against the crowds to his destination.
V25	Here we have the sick woman with a haemorrhage.
V26	She is obviously very sick. According to the law of Moses she is unclean.
	"If a woman has a flow of blood for several days outside her monthly period or if her flow continues beyond her regular period, she remains unclean as long as the flow continues, just as she is during her monthly period." (Leviticus 15: 25).
V27	She desperately wants to touch Jesus.
V28	She believes that if she can just touch Jesus she will be healed, because she is a woman of great *Faith*.
V29	She does manage to touch him and she knows immediately that she is healed.
V30	Even amidst this huge crowd Jesus stops and says that someone has 'touched him'. He is aware that *"Power has gone out of him"* and to get this message over to the people he has to reveal who it is.
V31	I think the disciples must have been rather amused at first, because everyone is pressing and touching him.
V32	The eyes of Jesus infiltrate the woman's heart.

V33   She is aware that Jesus knows it is her because of his gaze upon her. Although she is frightened, she comes forward, no doubt knowing of the message Jesus has to get over to the crowd. This message is that there are two different kinds of '*Touch*'.

(1) To Touch Him Physically.
(2) To Touch Him in *Faith*.

The physical 'touch' is not important, but if you 'touch' me in *Faith* then there will be a bond between us. This woman has touched him in *Faith*.

V34   He tells her with compassion that her *Faith* healed her.

V35   So there Jesus has another interruption, but his reaction is one of love for someone in need. However, during this time, the daughter of Jairus has died. Notice the lack of *Faith*.

V36   Have they not already seen what *Faith* can do? Yet Jesus has to remind them that anything is possible if you have *Faith*. Where there is *Faith* God can work.

V37   He takes with him the three disciples who are to witness his great miracles, his glory and his humiliation.

V38   When someone dies it is the Jewish custom and still is to-day with Orthodox Jews, to wail, which means to cry in sadness and people are often hired to do this for families.

V39   Jesus tells them that there is no reason for this as the child is only asleep.

V40   They laugh, not because it is funny, but because it is ridiculous to say that she is asleep when they have seen the dead girl and are capable of knowing when someone is dead or not. Why have they then brought in people to 'wail'? Anyway, nobody can raise the dead! These are the thoughts of the mourners. Therefore Jesus sends them away.

V41   Here again we see the tremendous *Love* and *Compassion* of Jesus. He gently takes the girl's hands into his own and quietly speaks to her in his own language, *Aramaic*. He says '*Talitha, Koum*' which means "Little Girl, I tell you to get up!"

V42   You can imagine the reaction of the people, especially those who laughed at him, when she got up! You can also understand that they are so overwhelmed by *God's Power* in this

situation that they cannot move or speak.
V43   They are so overwhelmed that they have forgotten that the child will be hungry. So Jesus reminds them.
Note that he asks them to keep quiet about this miracle. So here we have another example of the *Messianic Secret*.

Note

Up to now Jesus has only been preaching in and around *Galilee*.
In the next three chapters we see Jesus going further afield.

The word that is used in the Greek New Testament for *Power*, is *Dunamis* and it is used for:-

a) The *Power* of God.
b) The *Power* of the *Holy Spirit*.
c) *Power* that works through Jesus' *Miracles*.

When you are Baptised and Confirmed you are given the *Power* of the *Holy Spirit*, a form of *Dynamite*!
But God's *Dynamite* will only explode where there is great *Love* inside the *Heart*. You are *God's* instruments on earth and he wants you to be filled with *His Love*. So much so, that you will *Blast His Power* of *Love* on this *Earth*.
Ask yourself how do I show my Love of God?
How have I used the *Power he gave me*?
Have I blasted –
a) *Evil* into *Goodness* when I came up against it?
b) *Hatred* into *Love* when I saw people saying and doing hateful things?
c) *God's presence wherever I am*?

Questions Mark Chapter Five

1. Why does Satan recognise Jesus before man?
2. Give an account of Jesus healing a man with Evil Spirits.
3. Why does God not reveal his name to Moses?
4. Why does Satan not want to leave this place?
5. Why do you think the reaction of the people is one of fear?
6. Why does Jesus not ask the man to keep quiet?
7. Relate the story of the woman who is healed in *Faith*.
8. Who is healed by the 'touch' of Jesus?
9. Where do you find the lack of Faith in this chapter?
10. What is the reaction of these people?

St. Mark Chapter Six

Jesus is Rejected at Nazareth

V1   Here we see Jesus taking his disciples back to his own home, *Nazareth*, where he was brought up.

V2   Here Jesus is preaching to 'many people,' which indicates their interest in his teachings. There are people present who have grown up with him and all are aware of his work in *Galilee*. They wonder at his teachings, for indeed he is the 'Master Teacher' and how he can heal people. Their Faith is being tested!

V3   Although interested in his teachings they cannot accept Jesus as the *Messiah*, for they are spiritually blind! Therefore they fail the test of *Faith*. All they can see is 'the Carpenter' and not their *Saviour*! Because of their lack of *Faith* the people reject Jesus!

In reference to the words 'brother' and 'sisters' both in the Old and New Testaments these words have a much wider meaning than the way we use them! They mean relatives, cousins, or even followers.

V4   Jesus is saying here that prophets will find it hard to be accepted in their own home towns. "It was the will of the Lord that his servant should grow like a plant taking root in dry ground" (Isaiah 53: 2).

V5   He is unable to perform miracles because of the lack of *Faith*. There appears to be a few who do have *Faith* because Jesus heals some people.

V6   The people in general have failed to 'touch' Jesus in Faith, so therefore he can do little work in his own home town. They have failed to understand his words because they are spiritually deaf!; they have failed to see who he really is

because they are spiritually blind!

This should be a great lesson for us. We are so used to receiving the Sacraments, for example we can receive Holy Communion every day. Do we take this for granted? Or do we really reach out to Our Father and 'Touch Him in Faith?'

Jesus Sends out the Twelve Disciples

V7   The disciples have been with Jesus long enough to know what he would want them to preach to the people. Jesus sent them out in twos for that is the custom both in the Old Testament and in the early Church. Here Jesus gives them authority to cast out evil spirits.

V8-9   Now they are to be Apostles, 'sent ones,' and Jesus gives them certain instructions as to what they are to take with them on their journey. They are to rely on the compassion of people to give them bread to eat, for they are not to beg. What Jesus is really saying is that he wants them to really trust God, for then, God will not see them starve.

Here is another lesson for us! Jesus is aware that people go round saying that they trust God, but are they really honest with themselves? Is it not true that, faced with a serious situation where we put our trust in God, we sometimes need to have a good look at our spirituality and really work at it?

So Jesus wants his Apostles to do it so clearly and openly that it will open the eyes of the people so that they will see their own 'lack of trust' and do something about it.

V10   Stay and preach the 'Good News' about the Kingdom of God. They want to be saved!

V11   Here he tells them not to stay where they are not wanted. "Shake the dust off your feet" means that they have gone into that place as God's representatives to preach about the Kingdom of God.

But if man will not listen to the word of God, it is man's own downfall; his loss of Salvation; his loss of Eternal Life with God in Heaven. Man has been given his chance, therefore the Apostles can walk away for they have fulfilled their duty. We all have a serious responsibility to hear the word of God and live up to it, if we want to Save our Souls!

"After the seven days had passed, the Lord spoke to me. "Mortal man" he said, "I am making you a watchman for the nation of Israel. You will pass on to them the warnings I give you. If I announce that an evil man is going to die but you do not warn him to change his ways so that he can save his life, he will die still a sinner, and I will hold you responsible for his death. If you do warn an evil man and he does not stop sinning, he will die, still a sinner, but your life will be spared. If a truly good man starts doing evil, and I put him in a dangerous situation, he will die if you do not warn him. He will die because of his sins, I will not remember the good he did, and I will hold you responsible for his death. If you do warn a good man not to sin, and he listens to you and does not sin, he will stay alive, and your life will also be spared." (Ezekiel, "The Watchman", 3: 16-21).

V12   The first step towards Heaven is to Repent (Reconciliation) and that is what the disciples preached.

V13   Jesus gave them the power to cast out evil spirits and to anoint the sick with oil to heal them.

The Death of John the Baptist

V14   King Herod Antipas is the ruler of Galilee and hated by the people. He has heard all about the work and popularity of Jesus. He is also aware that the people are saying that John the Baptist has come alive and it is he who is performing these great wonders.

V15   The people are all talking about him and some say that he is like the prophets of old! Whenever the prophets of old spoke something always happened. The people are linking this with the miracles that they have heard about.

V16   Even Herod thinks that it is John the Baptist who has come back to life. Herod has always been aware that John has been sent by God and this always greatly disturbs him.

V17   Herod has arrested John and eventually has him put to death. This is because of Herodias, whom he has persuaded to divorce her husband, Herod's brother, and in turn Herod divorced his wife and married Herodias.

V18   John the Baptist tells Herod that he is committing a grave sin by marrying Herodias. God has sent John to Herod to give him the opportunity of repenting. Herod, it appears, always feels safe when John is around and perhaps he would have repented, but his lust for Herodias is too great and eventually Herodias wins.

V19   Here we see premeditated murder in the heart of Herodias. Herod will not have him put to death immediately, but keeps him in prison. Herod rather fears John because he knows that John is a very holy man.

V20   Herod listens to John, and his words greatly disturbed Herod's conscience. Later we see Pilate battling with his conscience. He does not condemn Jesus to death until he announces to the people three times that he is innocent. He eventually gives way to the demands of the people. Herod likes to hear the truth but he does not understand it because of the sinfulness in his life.

V21-25 This is a most horrific banquet. We see the quality of this banquet when Herodias's daughter asks for the Head of John the Baptist. We are aware of evilness in Herod, Herodias and her daughter. It is interesting to note that not one person at the banquet stood up in protest at the request. Is it because they are all of the same kind? This indeed is a *Banquet in Hell*.

If we look at the parable of the 'Wedding Feast' we see a *Banquet in Heaven*. We see Love, Joy, Peace and Happiness within the hearts of all the guests.

V26   This makes Herod distressed but really it is 'the fear of man', for Herod is proud, and he does not want 'to lose face' or his popularity with his guests. Herod does not 'fear God;' he is more concerned with what his guests will think of him if he refuses this evil request!

Is it not true that some people are afraid of going to Church, of even being seen in Church and of keeping God's laws because of what their friends will say about them. I have heard young people say "Don't tell the others that I went to church". They appear to be ashamed of their action. Do you realise that it is your *Faith* that is being tried and tested. Remember always what Jesus said, "If a person is ashamed of me and my teachings in this Godless and wicked day, then the *Son of Man* will be ashamed of him" (Mark 8: 38). There will be many

situations in your life where you will be tested, so be ready! Indeed your friends may well criticise you when you say that you cannot attend a football match because you have to go to Church. Perhaps you have to turn something down with your friends because you promised to do something in your Parish. There may well be an occasion when you refuse to watch a video because it is 'lustful' and full of filthy words and your friends will laugh at you! These people may well not understand because they are unbelievers. However your problem is your own soul and you are the only one who can save it! Remember that we have within us the gift of the Spirit, *'Fear of God'. 'The Fear of God' is the beginning of Wisdom and Participation in his Love. The fear of Man is a trap. Satan wants us all to fall into that 'Trap!'Stand firm in your Faith!*

V27   Herod gives John no time to prepare for his death, but we know that John is a very holy man. He spent his whole life in the service of God endeavouring to save as many souls as he could! He is a man of great courage and protests against *Evil* right up to the end of his life. His death is Satanic because it is a gift to two lustful women!

V28   Here you have a foreshadowing, a prediction of Calvary! Nothing could be more degrading or humiliating than that the only reason why you are to die, is due to the wishes of two evil women, who want your head to be placed on a plate and served into the banqueting hall. It was the custom in those days, when they served the meat, to place the head of the animal and decorate it up before taking it into the banquet! John does not have the chance of even dying a Martyr's death.

V29   The disciples came and buried the body of John. This is also another foreshadowing of Jesus. Jesus is aware of what is happening to John but he knows John would have to pay this great price!

"He will be a great man in the Lord's sight."

(Luke 1: 15).

Jesus realises that the aggression of evil is beginning to gather force against the Kingdom of God.

Jesus Feeds Five Thousand Men

V30   The Apostles report back to Jesus and are no doubt full of eagerness to tell him all about their mission.

V31   Here we see the crowds gathering again. So much so that they could not even eat, let alone have a conversation. Jesus is aware of the work they have done and that they need rest. He suggests to them that they should all go away and find peace and quiet in some lonely place, away from the crowds.

It is the will of God for all of us to work but also to take time off and rest. God says that there is time for everything! *(Read Ecclesiastes 3).*

V32   They set out to find a quiet place where they can rest, pray and talk.

V33   The people see them go and realise their destination. In fact they get there as Jesus and the disciples arrive.

V34   Again we see Jesus being interrupted. Although he must be under great pressure and in need of rest, he has no thought of self. He is filled with Love and Compassion for these people who are in need.

Not only does he teach them but he is also going to feed them.

V35   The disciples tell him how late it is.

V36   They suggest that Jesus tells them to go away and find shelter and something to eat.

V37   Here Jesus is giving them an Assignment for all time. He is telling them that their work will be to feed the people with the physical bread and to feed them with the *Spiritual Bread.* But they look at it from a purely *Human Situation* and start wondering how they can possibly afford to feed these people.

What they should have done was to say "Lord, this is impossible for us to do, but your *Power* can make it *Possible.* Give us the *Power* to do it."

This happens to us in situations that seem impossible, but if we turn to God for help, he will not let us down! It is man who lets God down by his unbelief and sinfulness.

V39   He tells his disciples to go and make the people comfortable.

V40   We are told that there are 5,000 people but there must be more, because the Jews never count the women and children!

V41 All Jesus has before him are five loaves and two fishes. Numbers in the Scriptures all have a symbolic meaning and five and two make 'seven'. The number seven is the perfect number.

V42 Thus when the five loaves and the two fishes are put into the hands of Jesus it becomes the perfect gift. Jesus blesses it and breaks it, and there is enough for everyone. The greatest problem in the world is *Us*. All that God wants is for *Man* to completely surrender himself to God. Then God can bless and break man and make him the 'Perfect Gift.'

V43-44 There are twelve baskets of food left. The number twelve represents the 'twelve tribes of Israel.' This symbolises that Jesus has enough food left to feed the whole Church!
When we surrender ourselves to God and he has blessed and broken us, he can then send us out to do his work, but it is the 'broken' part we do not like, for this means 'suffering.' Yet this path of being 'blessed and broken' will one day lead us to our 'Heavenly Home.'

Jesus Walks on the Water

V45 He sends his disciples to Bethsaida which is a fishing town on the north shore of Lake Galilee and the home of Peter, Andrew and Philip. Jesus sends them away because they are exhausted. He then dismisses the crowds.

V46 Jesus retires to a quiet place to speak with His Father on the hillside.

V47 Jesus sees the disciples struggling with the boat in the water. This is a picture of the Church today and Jesus on the hillside represents Jesus praying for us.

V48-50 This represents us struggling; we are in the boat of *Peter*, the *Church,* and instead of allowing him to rescue us we continue to toil against a head wind. The head wind represents all the opposition that we come up against in this world. He is there for us to reach out and touch him in Faith and he will come to our rescue; but are we spiritually blind?
The Lake represents 'History.' As the Church struggles through all the resistance and obstacles that come its way, we know that one day Jesus will return. This will be the 'Second Coming!'

We will not be frightened if we live according to his Laws. We must live out a life of love and holiness. We must turn away from anything that is evil.

For on that day man will have to reckon with *God*! However *Jesus* is standing by the throne of his *Father* interceding for us. The power that we need is there. All we have to do is ask for it! It is completely up to us!

V51   If we want the Church to have power and, remember, we are the *Church*, to combat all the *Evils* in this wicked world, then we must have *Jesus* in the boat with us and the wind will stop!

V52   They are 'amazed' for they have already seen the miracle of the loaves and now they see him coming in *Power*. They are beginning to realise that he has *Power* over everything!

Jesus Heals the Sick in Gennesaret

V53   They set off to the western side of Lake Galilee.

V54   The people notice Jesus getting out of the boat.

V55   Word quickly spreads of his arrival and all the sick are brought to him.

V56   You can see how widespread his popularity has become. Obviously the news of his great works have come to the ears of these people. Great crowds gather bringing their sick with them.

Notice again the word 'beg', for some just want to touch him, "at least touch the edge of his cloak." Those that do 'touch' him must have '*Faith*' for they are healed. People are beginning to realise the great power of Jesus and that he is no ordinary man!

Questions Mark Chapter Six

1. Why do you think Jesus is rejected in Nazareth?
2. Give an account of Jesus sending out the Twelve Disciples.
3. What is the difference between a 'Banquet in Heaven' and a 'Banquet in Hell?'
4. Give an account of the Death of John the Baptist.
5. Give an account of the Feeding of the Five Thousand.
6. What is the significance of the miracle, 'Jesus Walks on the Water,' for us?

St. Mark Chapter Seven

The Teaching of the Ancestors

V1   The Scribes and Pharisees must be getting extremely worried about the vast popularity of Jesus. We notice here that people have actually come up from Jerusalem to watch what he is doing.

V2   Now we are going to see Jesus once again coming into *Opposition* with the Scribes and Pharisees. The latter have noticed that Jesus' disciples are eating before they have washed their hands! Now we know that it is very hygienic to wash your hands before a meal, but the Jews do it because it is part of their religious Laws.

V3   The religious Law states that their hands should be washed before eating because they may have touched a Gentile or something that a Gentile had touched! This will make their hands 'unclean' and unfit to eat food, which they consider a gift from God. This Law is not according to Moses; it has been introduced by the Religious Leaders themselves.

V4   Again, anything bought at the market, whether it is meat or utensils, have to go through a ceremonial washing, as it may have been in contact with Gentiles and will therefore be 'unclean.' The Jew on his return from market will also have to wash his hands up to the elbow. To the Jew their hands will then be cleansed and consecrated, thus fit to eat the food that God has sent them.

Cups and plates are washed in a special way even after they have eaten. This ritual is still carried on today by Orthodox Jews.

V5   They ask Jesus why his disciples break the Law and eat with unclean hands.

V6-9   Jesus, as we know, has no *Fear of Man* and he is prepared to stand up to anyone with the *Truth*. So he says to them, "You are Hypocrites!" He tells them that God has no time for their 'Lip Service' or 'External Traditions'. That God is only interested in one thing and that is their *Heart*! Their rules and regulations have no meaning and their worship is therefore *Useless*. Jesus illustrates this when he mentions *Isaiah*.

The Lord said, "These people claim to worship me, but their words are meaningless, and their hearts are somewhere else. Their religion is nothing but human rules and traditions, which they have simply memorised." (Isaiah 29: 13).

Jesus tells them that they have simply made a mockery of the Commandments of God.

V10-12   Here he again illustrates by using the Fourth Commandment. "Respect your Father and Mother" means to look after them both physically and spiritually in their old age. The negative side of this Commandment is that anyone who curses his mother or father must be put to death. Jesus tells them that he knows what they are up to. People would say to their parents, 'I would love to help you but I cannot because I have given my money to the Temple.' *Corban* is an *Aramaic word* meaning *Dedicated to God*. This got them out of the responsibility of looking after their parents. The Jews have a fantastic way of getting round their obligations. They know that they have a duty to keep the *Fourth Commandment* and look after their parents, just as their parents have looked after them when they were born; but they turn their backs on them with this excuse. The Pharisees and many others who are following in their steps are saying 'I have given it all to the *Lord*, so the money is not mine anymore, it is the *Lord's* money, therefore I do not have any responsibility towards you!'

What a shock they get when Jesus tells them that there is no way that they can get around not *Obeying the Fourth Commandment of God*. Jesus tells them that the money that they gave to the Lord is now the Lord's money. But the Lord wants them to keep His Commandment! So they must take his money and go and take responsibility for their parents!

What Jesus is also saying is that they have accused him and his disciples of breaking their man made rules, but he is accusing them of breaking a *Major Commandment of God*!

V13   Notice the word *Many*. Jesus only gives them one example about their teachings, the *Fourth Commandment*, because he is full of compassion for all who suffer. Jesus knows that many elderly people are suffering greatly in *Israel* because of the misunderstanding of this tradition.

Here Jesus is speaking about Judaism having become far too legalistic. Their man made rules and regulations left no room for God.

The Things that Make a Person Unclean

V14   Here Jesus is referring to the whole of creation for all time.

V15-16 Jesus is saying here that what makes you unclean is what comes out of your *Heart*! It has nothing to do with the rules and regulations of touching things. When you went to the market, for example, to trade, this did not make you spiritually unclean!

V17   The disciples ask him to explain this to them.

V18-20 Jesus explains that it is not the things of the outside that make a man unclean. The Jews are not allowed to eat pigs, because they are considered dirty animals and they think that they will make them unclean. Jesus explains that it is not what goes into the mouth of a man, but rather what comes out of the mouth that makes him unclean.

Also food can either be clean or unclean only in the physical sense.

V21-23 Jesus explains that it is the *Heart* that is the *Centre of Man's Motivation*. The *Heart* makes you act and say the things that you do. It is from the *Heart* that *Evil* comes and makes you unclean. The *Heart* is the *Centre of Love* in a person and if it is given up to *God*, then only *Love* and *Goodness* will prevail. *God* wants you to have a *New Heart* and a *New Spirit*. Jesus tells them of some of the *Evil* things that are motivated by the *Heart*.

A Woman's Faith

V24   Jesus travels to the outskirts of the Phoenician City of Tyre. He is in need of rest and therefore looked for a place where no one would find him.

V25   However, a pagan woman and a foreigner, for she is Syro-Phoenician, probably born in Phoenicia and living in the region of Syria, found Jesus. She kneels before him, for she has Faith and she is in need, for her daughter is sick.

V26   This woman is also a Gentile. Notice the word begged. She obviously has the *Faith* to know that Jesus could send this evil spirit out of her daughter.

V27   These words sound rather harsh coming from Jesus but we must not forget that although he is God, he is man! Therefore as a man we must accept that he must have been extremely exhausted dealing with the huge crowds and the opposition from the religious teachers and is himself in great need of rest! Just as you or I would be! However it could be that he is testing the woman's *Faith*! The children here are the Jews for it is God's plan of *Salvation* to reach the hearts of people through the Jews. The Jew often refers to the Gentiles as 'dogs.' Jesus is sent to the Jews as the final Prophet, so it is God's will that he should preach the Gospel to the Jews first! The woman understands this.

V28   The woman is saying, 'Yes Lord, I understand but when the Jews throw away whatever God has given them or whatever parts of revelation they will share, others are ready to accept it.' This woman has great insight and is aware of Jesus' first duty and accepts that he is not keeping revelation back from the Gentiles. The 'Good News' is to be for the whole of mankind.

V29   Jesus is full of admiration at this woman's capacity to understand. He tells her, because her *Faith* is so great, to go home and she will find that her daughter is healed. This is one of the few healings that Jesus performed from a distance.

V30   The woman returns home to find her daughter completely healed.

Jesus Heals a Deaf Mute

V31   Jesus leaves Tyre and makes his way back to Lake Galilee, passing through *Decapolis, Greek* for *Ten Towns.* This is the place where he had healed the 'Man with *Evil Spirits.'*

V32   Notice again the word 'begged.' These people have brought this man who is deaf and finds difficulty in speaking, because they know that Jesus can make him well again. Is this not symbolic of the healing that we all need? Are our ears open to the word of God? Do we really listen to the word of God during our Scripture Lessons?

Are our *Hearts* really open and do we really let *His Words Penetrate* and touch us?

If it is true that we have difficulty in hearing God's word, then would it not be true to say that we obviously would not be able to preach it, or at least we would find it very difficult! When your friends bring up religion and start talking about God, what is your reaction when they start asking questions? Do you make an excuse and leave their company? Do you just sit in silence and listen? Do you just go along with anything they say because you do not know the answers? Do you agree with something they say, like 'You do not have to go to Church it, is boring.' 'Religion is stupid!' 'Let us have a good time while we can'. You know what I am talking about because there have been times when you were in that kind of situation! Are you *Afraid of Man* and do not have the *'Fear of God'* which means fear of losing *God's Love! His Wisdom! Remember* Chapter 6: 26.

V33   Jesus takes this man away from the crowd to see to his needs privately.

"The blind will be able to see, and the deaf will hear" (Isaiah 35: 5).

This way we all need to go to God privately in our prayers to take away our blindness, our deafness and let him touch our hearts in *Faith.* Then God will give us the answers to the questions that our friends ask. No longer will we remain silent in the *Fear of Man,* for God will give us *Wisdom, Knowledge and Understanding.*

Is there also another lesson for us here. When Jesus takes this man away from the crowd, he speaks and prays with him. In other words he *Communicates* with him. Then he heals him, so that he can also *Communicate* with other people. Now, how well do you *Communicate* with your family, friends and neighbours? Have you ever realised that families to-day are being destroyed because of lack of *Communication* between each other. It may well be that the family have been out at school or at work and feel they want a little bit of peace when they get home. But what about mum? She may have been in the house all day with no one to speak to! When she speaks to you is there 'silence', or 'just a minute', or does the 'minute' go into 'hours'? What is the reaction in your family when someone wants to share something? It could be a problem they have, or it could be something pleasant that they want to share. Do you realise, no matter how tired, or concerned you are with your own thoughts, you can be extemely hurtful to those around you, when you fail to communicate?

Lack of communication between people can leave a feeling of rejection, which can result in the destruction of an individual's personality. God wants us to be good listeners and communicate in a positive way! Therefore let your home, school, or work be places filled with happy conversations. Do not let *Satan's Silence Spread* into your life and become the signpost of your home, school or work! Life is short; love one another and converse with love in your heart. Speak, as if you were speaking to Jesus. Remember even a smile is a form of prayer.

V34 Jesus gives a deep sigh. He cries out, *'EPHPHATHA,'* an *Aramaic* word meaning *"Open Up."* Why did Jesus 'sigh?' Because he is very sad at our weakness to hear the word of God and to preach it. We are to be *God's* instruments, *His Witnesses* in this world. Without knowing the 'Word of God' how can we do this?

St. Paul tells us that *Faith* comes to us by hearing and hearing comes from the word of God being *Preached*. So if we let the word go into our *Hearts, Faith* will be stirred up within us. Then *God* can really work inside of us!

V35 The man is healed. He can speak without any difficulty.

V36 Jesus requests them not to tell anyone about this miracle, but they go and spread the news. Here again, we find evidence of the *Messianic Secret*.

We know that Jesus wants to keep this a secret for the time has not yet come for this to be revealed to the people. He does not want to be considered as a political leader or great healer, for this is not why he has been sent.

V37   Everyone is, note the word, 'Amazed', also note that they compliment how well he does his work!

Questions Mark Chapter Seven

1. Why do the Scribes and Pharisees come into *Opposition* with Jesus?
2.   How does Jesus answer them?
3. Give an account of Jesus explaining the Fourth Commandment and the 'Corban.'
4. What makes a person unclean according to the teaching of Jesus?
5. Relate the story of the woman's Faith.
6. What do you understand by Spiritual Blindness and Spiritual Deafness?
7. Why is it so very important to communicate with God, our families and neighbours?

St. Mark Chapter Eight

Jesus Feeds Four Thousand People

V1   Another large group of people come to listen to Jesus but before long they have no food left and they are hungry. Jesus gathers his disciples around him.

V2   Here again we see the compassion of Jesus for his people. He tells the disciples that he feels sorry for them.

V3   His great popularity has brought multitudes to listen to him from far and wide. They have listened to the teachings of Jesus for three days and have run out of food. They are so eager to find Jesus that they forget about food. Jesus is aware that they are not fit to travel back home without first being fed.

V4   The disciples want to know where they will find food? They appear to have forgotten the 'Miracle of the Loaves' very quickly. (6: 30-44)

V5   They have *seven loaves*. Remember the perfect number, the perfect gift.

V6-9   So we have the *second miracle* of the loaves. Here again Jesus is going to take the loaves and later the fish, into his hands and he will bless it and break it. There is enough food to feed Four Thousand people. The food that is left over would be enough to feed his whole Church. Jesus is foreshadowing Calvary when he himself will be 'broken.' This great sacrifice will 'feed' his people until the end of time. It is to be our Spiritual Food!

V10   Jesus goes to Dalmanutha.

The Pharisees Ask for a Miracle

V11 Here Jesus comes up against more *opposition* and criticism from the Pharisees. They want to 'trap' him if they can, for that has been their main aim from the start. They ask Jesus to give them 'a sign'. Yet they have experienced, already, many signs, for example:-
The deaf can hear.
The lame can walk.
The dead have been raised.
The evil spirits cast out.
The hungry have been fed.
They could not accept this because of their total 'blindness' and their unbelief! I doubt that even if Jesus had raised a 'mountain into the air', they still would **not** have believed. Their hearts were utterly closed!

V12 Jesus refuses. In Luke 2: 33 we are told that it is because the 'sign' is in front of them 'Jesus, Himself', but they are so 'spiritually blind' they cannot see it! Jesus realises that he is up against Judaism. So he tells the disciples and the people to keep away from the influence of the Scribes and Pharisees. Jesus wants people to come to Him in *Faith!*
Why does Jesus give a 'deep groan'? It is because Jesus suffered greatly for he saw the:-
a) Lack of *Faith* in *Man. His unbelief.*
and
b) The stubbornness in their hearts. What they have heard and seen has only fallen on 'Stubborn Hearts' and 'Deaf Ears.'

V13 Jesus leaves them abruptly, gets into the boat and goes to the other side of the Lake with his disciples.

The Yeast of the Pharisees and of Herod

V14 The disciples have forgotten to take enough food with them, but they have the 'bread of life' in the boat with them, so they have no cause to worry.

V15 Why does he use the word 'yeast'? Yeast is normally a symbol of *Evil* in parables, but not in some of the parables! Yeast is considered to be an influence. It can either be good or bad.

We know that yeast makes our bread rise when it is being cooked. We cannot hear or see what the yeast is doing until we have the final result, the Loaf! But Jesus says 'take care.' He is warning them that they are up against Bad Influence. For Herod is a very immoral man; a worldly man; a stubborn and unbelieving man; this is his Yeast!

The Pharisees' Yeast could be said to be:-

Hypocrisy.
Unrepentant Hearts.
Pride.
Bigotry.
Ritualism.

They also have premeditated murder in their hearts.

So Jesus is saying 'be careful,' for these things destroy a man's life.

V16   All the disciples can think about is their dinner and their minds are not on what Jesus is talking about!

V17-20 Jesus is really asking them if they have already forgotten how he fed the multitudes in the desert? He asks them questions and they answer him concerning the miracle of the Five Thousand. Jesus must have felt extremely sad for he can see that his disciples are still 'spiritually deaf' and 'spiritually blind.'

V21   Here Jesus is trying to get his disciples to face up to their 'spiritual blindness.' They have witnessed his miracles, so it seems incredible that they can sit and worry about their 'dinner!'

Even so, miracles are happening to-day, but there are still many people, though they see the miracle, just cannot believe what has happened!

Now Jesus is going to move into a situation of healing a blind man. As Jesus heals this man of his physical blindness he is also saying to his disciples that he wants to heal them all of their 'spiritual blindness!'

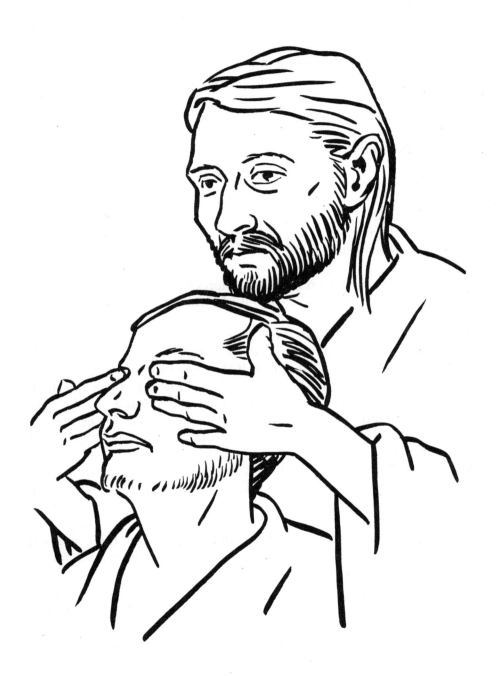

Jesus Heals a Blind Man at Bethsaida

V22   Jesus and his disciples go to Bethsaida on the northern shore
       of Lake Galilee. Here the people bring a blind man and beg
       Jesus to heal him.
V23   Saliva is an outward sign of healing.
V24   Notice that in this miracle there are two stages of healing.
       Normally the healings of Jesus are immediate, but Jesus has
       his own reasons for healing this man in the way he does, as we
       shall see later!
       However we can consider this as a lesson in 'Loving our
       Neighbour.' Do we see our neighbour's problems? Do our
       neighbours see our problems?
       Do we see people's needs clearly? Or do we just dismiss what
       we see because it will mean becoming involved. We will have
       to go to their needs and this will involve us giving of our time!
       Some do not like giving of their time because they are very
       self-centred and their time is very precious to them! We should
       all be aware of each other, love each other and reach out to
       each other. In this way we feed each other with God's
       presence. This is the Will of God. In our Spiritual lives we are
       touched by God in our Baptism and again in our Confirma-
       tion. However, he gives us free will to choose whichever path
       we want. I think that it is true to say that as we walk along the
       spritual path of life, we are all in continual need of His Loving
       Touch!
V25   We can see that Jesus has healed this man slowly and
       gradually. The man can now see clearly! Jesus here is showing
       his disciples that only very slowly and gradually are they
       beginning to see who Jesus really is! Indeed, they are very
       slow!!
V26   Jesus tells the man not to go and tell people. He wants to keep
       it quiet. Here again is evidence of the '*Messianic Secret.*'

Peter's Declaration about Jesus

We now come to what is called the 'Hinge Question.'
We are about half-way through Mark's Gospel and now we

come in this event, to the turning point! There are earlier hints about Jesus' death but now Jesus starts to prepare his disciples for what he knows must be his destiny, "His Father's will."

V27-28 On their way to Caesarea Philippi Jesus, in conversation, asks them who the people think he is? The disciples tell him what the people are saying about him. Most certainly the disciples themselves should have been able to answer that 'question', because they have heard his teachings and experienced his miracles. But they are, as we know 'spiritually blind', yet Jesus has revealed that they are growing, although very slowly, towards the *Truth* of who he is!

Although Jesus tells the people to keep quiet about his works, he knows that they fail to do this.

Again we can appreciate why he wants *His Messiahship to be kept a secret* from the people because:-

a) It will endanger his Ministry.

b) The people expect a *Messiah* who will supply their material needs.

c) They expect a *Messiah* who will destroy the Romans "You have defeated the Nation that oppressed and exploited your people." (Isaiah 9: 4).

d) They expect a *Messiah*, who will be like an earthly King going to war with an army and defeating other Nations. (Read, Isaiah 11: 10-16).

e) The Romans will consider his claim as a *Jewish King*, a *Political* threat to Roman Power. Later we will see what Jesus says about the *True Messiahship*.

V29 This question is not just for Peter and the rest of the Apostles, it is for all disciples until the end of time! On our Confirmation Day we make a personal commitment to be *His Witness* in this world. We are his hands, his feet, his ears and his eyes, and he wants us to continue his work on this earth!

Peter answers Jesus and says, "You are the Messiah." The *Messiah*' meant 'the anointed one' in Hebrew. '*Christos*' is the Greek word and in English it is '*Christ*.'

We see here the turning point for this is the first time anyone has called *Him 'Messiah.'* Jesus is in complete admiration of

Peter because his 'blindness' has been absolutely inconceivable! Even though he wants them to know who he really is, Jesus asks them to keep quiet about it.

His Ministry in Galilee is almost finished and the journey to Jerusalem is about to begin. He therefore begins to prepare his disciples and gives them three prophecies of the *Passion*.

One in Chapter 8.
One in Chapter 9.
One in Chapter 10.

Jesus Speaks about His Suffering and Death

V31   Jesus speaks to his disciples about the *True Messiah*. He tells them that the Messiah will fulfil the prophecy of Isaiah: 53. He tells them that he will suffer grievously and will give his life in atonement for the sins of mankind; but that His Father will raise him up on the third day.

Now the Jews have two schools of thought about the prophecy of the coming Messiah. One is that he is going to be a Great King, who will sit on the throne of David and will be King forever. That he will be victorious and kill off all his enemies. The other school of thought, which they will not accept, is the Messiah who will suffer and die for man's sins. We know the path Jesus has chosen to walk and he fulfills all the prophecies about King David. He becomes not an earthly King but the King of Kings! He does His Father's will!

"We despised him and rejected him;
he endured suffering and pain."
(Isaiah 53: 3).
"But because of our sins he was wounded,
beaten because of the evil we did.
We are healed by the punishment he suffered,
made whole by the blows he received."
(Isaiah 53: 5).
"He was arrested and sentenced and led off
to die, and no one cared about his fate.
He was put to death for the sins of our people."
(Isaiah 53: 8).

"My devoted Servant, with whom I am pleased,
will bear the punishment of many and for his sake
I will forgive them."
(Isaiah 53: 11).

V32   Peter, hearing all this, and after realising that Jesus was the *Messiah*, just could not take it! He shows his disapproval to Jesus, and asks him not to go through with it! Poor Peter, his love for Jesus is so great that his human side comes out and he is 'spiritually blind' again. He cannot bear the thought of this happening to Jesus.

V33   Therefore Jesus has to bring Peter back on a spiritual level. He tells him off very severely because he wants Peter to realise that if we allow our feelings to prevent us from fulfilling God's Law then we are pleasing Satan and not God! To fulfil the Law of God in our lives is the most perfect thing we can do!

V34   Here Jesus tells his disciples, and also the crowd, that if they want to be his followers, his witnesses, they too will have to suffer! They will have to die to 'self'. This lesson is also for **Us**! This means that to live God's Law in your life you must become unselfish and reject or protest against many issues in Society that are not of God!

You must not be self-centred, thinking only of yourself and worldly things. Christ must be in the centre of your heart because that is the only way that you will be able to 'serve' him and your 'neighbour.' Many of his followers did die physically for their *Faith*. Even in this present day people like Maximillian Kolbe gave his life willing for the love of God and his neighbour. People like Mother Teresa have most certainly died to 'Self' and live only in the footsteps of Jesus by looking after those in 'great need.'

As his followers on earth, he wants us to 'live' his word, set the example within our community, family and at work. As individuals we must show responsibility, concern and love for all men!

"Do not let evil people worry you, do not be envious of them. A wicked person has no future, nothing to look forward to."
(Proverbs 29: 19-20).

123

V35   If you use your life only for worldly things then you will suffer a Heavenly loss; but those who let the Kingdom of God come into their lives and live and preach the word will enter God's Heavenly Home.

V36   You must make the choice! You can live a worldly life and stay 'spiritually blind,' but eventually you must suffer the consequences of rejecting complete happiness with God in Heaven for all eternity. Jesus asks us what is the use of being great or successful on earth if it means losing the only thing you possess, your own soul. There is no *price* that you can put on a *soul*!

V37   Jesus has shown us the way to Eternal Life with him in Heaven. He has told us that we must 'live' the word of God! There is no other way and we cannot just 'pick' and 'choose' what we want. Either we follow him and do as he says or we follow Satan.

V38   Very clear statement. If we are ashamed of Jesus in this world, and that means failing to do his work and failing to live as committed Christians, then he will be ashamed of us when we stand before His Father when we die.

Questions Mark Chapter Eight

1. Give an account of the Second Miracle of the Loaves.
2. Why do the Pharisees ask for a miracle?
   Why do you think Jesus refused?
3. Explain what you understand by the word 'yeast.' Give examples to explain your answer.
4. Why does Jesus heal this man in two stages?
5. Why does Jesus want *His Messiahship* to be kept a secret?
6. What question does Jesus put to Peter and what is his answer?
7. What does Jesus tell the disciples about his Passion. Why do you think Jesus tells them?
8. What does Jesus tell us about being His witnesses on this earth?
9. What is the choice we have to make in our lives?

St. Mark Chapter Nine

The Transfiguration

V1 Now that Jesus has shown them what is required of anyone who wishes to follow him, it is the most suitable time to allow them to see him in *His Glory*! The reason why Jesus does this is because he knows his disciples! He knows that they are going to witness his death on Calvary and it will be extremely hard for them to accept this terrible suffering and remember that he is the *Messiah*. So he is going to let them see this vision that they will never forget and also strengthen their *Faith*!

V2 Jesus takes Peter, James and John up the mountain with him. It is probably Mount Hermon because it is near Caesarea Philippi. Notice that whenever Jesus wants to be with God, he goes to a quiet place, away from the crowds, either by himself or takes some or all of his disciples with him. This occurs a number of times in the gospel.

V3 The word 'Transfiguration' means 'change of appearance.' Jesus lets the divine glory of God shine through him, but it is impossible to describe such a vision in human terms.

V4 Moses represents the Jewish Law, the great Lawgiver of the Old Testament. Elijah represents the Prophets. Thus they can see in this vision that Jesus is the fulfilment of the Law and the Prophets which is the foundation of the Jewish Religion. Jesus is speaking with them no doubt about the events that are to fulfil the prophecy of *Isaiah, His Death and Resurrection*.

V5 Peter is so amazed and fascinated at this great wonder that he wants to stay and he tells Jesus that he will prepare shelters for them. Can you see that he is putting Jesus, Moses and Elijah on the same level and so God has to intervene?

V6   There is fear in their hearts for they have never experienced such great wonder before.

V7   God intervenes and sends a cloud which covers Moses and Elijah. Then he points to Jesus and says "This is my own dear Son; listen to him!" God is telling them that Jesus is His Son and well above the Law of Moses and the Prophet Elijah. In other words *Jesus* is the *Messiah* so listen carefully to *His Words!*

V8   The vision has gone and Jesus is standing there as an ordinary human being. Do we see Jesus in our neighbour?

V9-13 Jesus tells them to keep quiet about the vision until His Resurrection. They obey him but they do not understand about the Resurrection. They ask him questions. Jesus tells them that Elijah has come in the person of John the Baptist and that as he has been put to death, so will the *Son* of *Man* suffer, for this is what the Scriptures state:-

"And so I will give him a place of honour, a place among great and powerful men. He willingly gave his life and shared the fate of evil men. He took the place of many sinners and prayed that they might be forgiven."
(Isaiah 53: 12).

Jesus Heals a Boy with an Evil Spirit

V14-15 They come down from the mountain to find the rest of the disciples. There is a crowd and some Pharisees and an argument is going on. But when the crowd see Jesus they run to him. This is the only time in the gospels that the people run to him in great surprise. They are looking at Jesus in amazement. Why? Because the 'Glory of God' is still over him and for the first time they catch a quick glimpse of who he really is. The crowd are overwhelmed and yet the disciples did not even notice. Mark here wants you to look back into the Old Testament when Moses went up Mount Sinai and spent forty days with God.

It is here that the 'Glory of God' is revealed to him and when he comes down from the mountain the 'Glory of God' is still over him. So much so, that the people cannot even look into his face, so Moses "Covered his face with a veil." (Exodus 34: 33).

V16 Jesus brings them down to earth and asks them why they are arguing.

V17 The boy suffers from epilepsy but has an evil spirit in him which makes him dumb.

V18 The disciples have been asked to heal this child and this attempt is not the first occasion for Jesus had given them power to heal (Mark 6: 13).

V19 Is his patience being tested? Yet we see that Jesus has the patience to see to the needs of this boy, even though he must be extremely exhausted. Note that Jesus can at times get angry, but it is not a weakness, rather his strength. For Jesus always spoke the *Truth* and his words are always righteous!

V20 Hear again it is the evil spirit who recognises Jesus and not the boy. The evil spirit starts to show off his power within the boy, but Jesus ignores him.

V21 Jesus speaks to the boy's father.

V22 When evil spirits are within a human being they are there obviously to do as much wickedness as they possibly can. Their work is purely to destroy, not only our physical being, but also our spirituality.

V23 Jesus here is telling the father that anything is possible if you have *Faith*. Jesus is really saying to the father that there is nothing wrong with the boy. He can be healed, but the father must believe and have *Faith*.

V24 This is the problem, the father lacks Faith! Is this not our problem also? The father asks Jesus to take away anything from him that is stopping the miracle from taking place. When we have problems do we make this request to Jesus?

V25 Notice the words "never go into him again!" Does this not show that there is a possibility of evil spirits entering a person again? Jesus here gives even more than the father asks for he leaves the boy spiritually free for the rest of his life.

V26 The evil spirit tries to draw attention to its power and everyone thinks that the boy is dead.

V27 Jesus takes his hand and the boy stands up. Remember that whatever you ask of God he will give you if you ask in Faith. However God will never give you something that he knows will harm you and God knows what is best for us all.

V28   The disciples show great concern as to why they could not heal the boy.

V29   Jesus tells them that to be his instruments on this earth, then there is a price to be paid. Notice the words 'this kind.' Is Jesus saying that there are certain kinds of 'Evil Spirits' that are more difficult to 'cast out' and therefore great prayer and fasting are required to exorcise these demons? I think that he is saying this to the disciples.

Jesus Speaks Again about His Death

V30   They travel through Galilee and Jesus desires his own privacy with his disciples.

V31-32 He wants to be alone with the disciples because for the second time he is going to prepare them for his death and Resurrection. He tells them what is going to happen to him. Notice he uses the words 'Son of Man.'
Because Jesus always speaks the truth, the prophecy actually happens. However the disciples do not want to accept what he is trying to tell them and they do not fully understand!

Who is the Greatest

V33-34 It is incredible to realise that Jesus has just been talking to them about *His Passion*, and now as they walk towards Capernaum, for Jesus is on his way to *Jerusalem*, they are arguing as to who will be the greatest! One would have thought that they would have been discussing what they would do when this terrible event occurreds. Perhaps they were living in a dream that Jesus' Kingdom would be just an earthly one. Have they deliberately closed their hearts and minds to what he is teaching them because it is too horrific for them to take in? In fact, although Jesus repeatedly speaks to them about the Passion, it is not until after the Resurrection that they fully understand!

V35   Jesus gathers them together. He knows what they have been talking about. So he tells them that to be the greatest you have to be the least of all! You have, in fact, to become a servant and serve.

V36-37 The disciples do not understand what he is trying to get over to them. So Jesus puts his arm around a little child to explain further.

He tells them that they may well think that they are great, but it is the attitude of this little child that is great and so very important in his sight. The child's attitude towards its father must be one of trust and complete dependence. So the message that Jesus is giving them and us, is that to be Great in God's sight we must be His Servant and Serve. We must be His Servant and Love. We must be His Servant and Trust. We must be His Servant in Faith.

In all things we must do the will of the Father! The child is an excellent example for Jesus to use as he is considered of no great importance to the Jews. The only great occasion is the time when a boy reached the age for his Bar Mitzvah and then became a man. Just consider the great work done to-day by people who serve! There are people who look after children in the N.S.P.C.C. There are people who voluntarily give of their time to care for sick and homeless children. There are many organisations where people care and love those who have been rejected, treated cruelly, homeless, starving and sick.

We do not have to be in an organisation to serve. God expects us to serve wherever we are, at home, at school or at work. We serve by behaving in a way that is pleasing to God, in our words and in our actions. This is the path to greatness.

Whoever Is Not against Us Is for Us

V38-41 Notice the words that John uses, "He does not belong to our group." Now, we know that one of the things Jesus accuses the Jews of is 'bigotry.' It is not God's will that we should be prejudiced against people of other creeds or colour, or that people should be persecuted because they are not of 'our group', or the other way around! God is much greater than our denominational problems, than the barriers that we put up to separate ourselves from each other.

Jesus here is showing that God looks at things differently to us. He is also telling them not to worry, "For whoever is not against us is for us" and whoever "gives you a drink of water

because you belong to me will certainly receive his reward."
The latter illustration that Jesus uses is interesting because we
have plenty of water, but where Jesus is, it is very scarce.
Therefore for someone to offer them a drink is a great
sacrifice, which God will remember! Whenever you do something for your neighbour out of *Love*, whether it is a smile, a
kind word or a helping hand it will never go unnoticed by God.
In fact, it is the greatest way of showing God how much you
love Him.

Temptations to Sin

Jesus gives us a very Solemn Warning! We make the choice:-
Heaven – Self-discipline
or
Hell – Self-ruin

V42   Jesus tells us that if we cause someone who lives a life of faith
to sin, or lose his faith ,it would be better for us to have
drowned in the sea.

V43   Hands can commit sinful actions or deeds. Cut the **sin** out of
your life! Take control of yourself.

V45   Feet can make you commit **sin.** They can take you into Evil
places or company. Cut the **sin** out of your life! Refuse to go.
Turn away from bad company! Do not be influenced. Be your
own master and have the courage to say No!!! Remember the
yeast, bad or good influence!

V47   Eyes can make you commit **sin.** They can make you have sinful
desires cut the **sin** out of your life!
Even the way you think or speak can be sinful it can not only
destroy you, but also other people. Do your words hurt your
family, your friends or your neighbour?
Are your thoughts lustful or offensive? Jesus is truly warning
us that we must not lead others into sin and we must not allow
ourselves to sin. Sin must be cut out of our hearts, or we must
suffer the consequences!

V48   The consequences are Hell Fire.
Now people do not like the word "Hell" and they do not like
to hear people talking about it. Why? Because they know that
sin has crept into their lives and they are enjoying it! They do

not want to believe that *Hell exists* because it would mean that they would have to *repent* and *change* their way of life. Well, God will not change to suit us! God does not change at all! God said:-

"As they leave, they will see the dead bodies of those who have rebelled against me. The worms that eat them will never die, and the fire that burns them will never be put out. The sight of them will be disgusting to all mankind."

'Rebelled' means sinned against God.

V49 In olden times salt was used to preserve meat and it was also used to purify wounds. Therefore salt is used for preservation and purification purposes.

V50 Jesus here is saying that he wants his disciples, us, to purify the earth and not to be contaminated by the World. We are meant to let the light of God shine through our lives. "You are the salt of the earth", means that God wants you to 'by allowing' the Kingdom of God to live in your Heart; then people can look at you and know that God really lives.

You are His witnesses on the earth. But if you lose your Grace by sinfulness you are of no use to God or Man. It is like salt losing its saltiness, you no longer preserve the world from sin, just as salt no longer preserves food. You are being contaminated by the world, living a life of sin and you become like flavourless salt!

I think that if we allow the words of Jesus to touch our hearts we must all agree that:–

To Live in Love,
To Live in Peace
To Live in Humility
To Live Generously
To Live Kindly

This would bring nothing but happiness to us all, we would have Heaven on Earth:-

The opposites of the above are what Satan wants. Hell on Earth, and 'In Eternity.' What do you want? But always remember that if you do fall, 'God is there to pick you up again and set you on the right road to Heaven! He gives us in Love, 'The Sacrament of Reconciliation.' Sinners can go to God and open up their hearts to him. His love is so great that he will forgive anyone who is truly sorry for having offended him in any way.

God loves you so much that He does not want anyone to hurt you or you to hurt anyone else. We are His children and He wants His Goodness, His Love to reign on this earth. It starts with you and me. Can you see the wisdom behind this?

Questions Mark Chapter Nine

1. What does the word Transfiguration mean?
2. What happens when they go up the mountain?
3. Why does Jesus do this?
4. Give an account of Jesus healing the boy with an evil spirit.
5. Why does he want to be alone with his disciples?
6. How does Jesus answer their question on 'Who will be the greatest?'
7. What answer does Jesus give to John concerning people who speak in his name?
8. What lesson is Jesus giving us here about the temptations to sin? Why does he refer to salt?

St. Mark Chapter Ten

Jesus Teaches about Divorce

V1   Jesus leaves Capernaum and makes his way to the province of Judea. He is making his way towards Jerusalem where he will suffer and eventually die to save all mankind. Crowds are waiting to listen to his teachings.

V2   The Rabbis have two schools of thought concerning Marriage and Divorce.

1 Some think that a man can divorce his wife just because he finds that he does not like something about her.

2 Others think that divorce is only right when adultery has been committed.

The Pharisees should not have asked this question because they are the leaders of the Law and they hold the authority within the Jewish Religion. However, they are aware that Jesus knows this, but they know that Jesus is claiming to come from God and to have God's authority. They are therefore challenging His Knowledge.

V3   Jesus is the 'Master Teacher' and he puts them in a 'trap.' He does not say "What did my Father *Command* you?"

He gets them to say what *Moses* has said, before he tells them what *His Father has Commanded*! Moses is the great Lawgiver in the Old Testament and God has given the *Ten Commandments* to Moses for his people to keep. The Jews accept Moses as the highest authority.

Notice the word *'Command'* and *'Permission.'*

V4   They say "Moses gave *Permission*."

There is a very great difference in *Commanding* something and giving *Permission*.

You might give permission to someone to do something,

  although it is against your better judgement, simply because
  you cannot persuade them to do the right thing and they just
  will not listen! This often happens in families between parents
  and teenagers.

V5   Here Jesus is telling them that Moses gave them permission
     because they are so unteachable! They do not want to hear the
     truth.

V6   Jesus reminds them that Marriage is God's idea and quotes
     from (*Genesis* 2: 24-25).

V7   Notice the words "Will leave," and note that they come before
     the words, "The two will become one."
     Jesus is saying here that *Sex* before *Marriage* is *Absolutely*
     against the *Law of God*!

V8   Therefore because they are one body and you cannot divide
     one body into two, then divorce is totally out.

V9   However, we are aware that in to-day's society people do get
     divorced for a number of reasons. Yet those who follow the
     word of God will not re-marry, for they still believe in
     the Sacredness of Marriage. They still believe that they are
     married in the eyes of God and only the death of one of the
     partners will give them the freedom, if they wish, to marry
     again. In the Roman Catholic Church where people have been
     granted an annulment they are free to remarry.

V10-12 In both cases adultery is committed! Therefore *Marriage* is a
     Holy and Sacred Bond and should be taken very seriously, be-
     cause both the man and the woman commit themselves totally
     to one another for life.

Jesus Blesses Little Children

V13-16 It is interesting to see that after his teaching on Marriage
     children are brought to him. Children are wonderful gifts from
     God. Parents are there to love, protect, give them security and
     good example. When Jesus hears the disciples reprimanding
     the people for bringing them to him he is angry! In the eyes of
     Jesus, children are utterly precious. He tells the people to
     bring them to him to be blessed. He says that the Kingdom of
     Heaven is for people like this. He is referring to the 'in-
     nocence' of a child. The opposite is being guilty of sin!

The Rich Man

V17   Notice the words the rich man uses. "What must I do?" Not "What must I be?"
Jesus is going to show this young man that to gain 'eternal life' he must change.

V18   Jesus here is challenging the young man as to who he is. Had the young man recognised that he is the Messiah it would have been a tremendous step towards *Faith*, but he does not see Jesus as the Messiah.

The Ten Commandments Given to Moses

Exodus 20: V1-V17

Note
1. Worship no God but me.
Do not make for yourself images of anything in Heaven or on Earth. Do not bow down to any idol or worship it.
2. Do not use my name for evil purposes, for I, the Lord your God will punish anyone who misuses my name.
3. Observe the Sabbath and keep it holy. You have *Six Days* in which to work but the *Seventh* day is a day of rest dedicated to me.
4. Respect your father and mother. The only commandment that promises long life to those who keep it.
5. Do not commit murder.
6. Do not commit adultery.
7. Do not steal.
8. Do not accuse anyone falsely.
9. Do not desire another man's wife.
10. Do not desire another man's house; do not desire his slaves, his cattle, his donkey or anything else that he owns.

   The first three are about God himself.
   The other seven are about our neighbours.

V19   Notice that the first three Commandments God gave are about

139

himself. Here Jesus speaks about the Commandments which refer to our neighbour. Jesus is not saying to the young man 'you do not love God'; he is saying "Do you love your neighbour?"

V20   He has all the material wealth and a good home. But Jesus knows that his problem is 'Love of one's neighbour.'

V21   Jesus looks at him and gives him a challenge and that is to go and show how much he really does love his neighbour. Now, this man loves his very comfortable life and it would be a great price for him to give all his wealth away! It is a great chance for him to step into *Faith* and follow Jesus because there is so much poverty around him.

V22   But he fails the test. What a wonderful chance he misses of changing his worldly wealth into Heavenly Wealth!

Remember, we too are being challenged in this way.

V23   Jesus is saying here that there is nothing wrong in having money. The thing that is wrong is when man puts all his love and security into it.

If you have a lot of money you have power in this world, you have influence. Remember the yeast. But money has no influence over God!

So if you ever get a lot of money, take up the challenge and see to those in need!

V24   Here Jesus is speaking about those people who really do put all their security in money and not in God. They are so spirtiually blind, like the rich man, that they cannot break away from it.

V25   Jesus is not saying that rich men will not enter into Heaven as the phrase would suggest. For Joseph of Arimathea is a Prince, Nicodemus and Zacchaeus are rich men. Indeed, many rich people have followed Jesus and some are now Saints, for example St. Francis of Assisi. This phrase means one of two things: – The old city of Jerusalem is a small city and you can walk from one end to the other in about twenty five minutes. The gates of the city have huge wooden doors and in the evening the traffic is only allowed to go down one street. At about 5.30 in the evening they close the city gates. There is a small, little door for pedestrians to go through and it is called 'the needle's eye.' A camel would certainly never get through.

The second possible explanation is the type of rope that they put round the camel's neck.

This rope is extremely thick and you would not think of trying to put it through an ordinary sewing needle!

The poor in God's eyes are not people who are destitute in the sense that they have no materialistic goods. God wants us to have money to see to our needs. A poor person in God's sight is someone who puts all his security into money and rejects the need for God in his own life!

V26   The disciples are getting worried as to who will enter the Kingdom of God.

V27   Here Jesus is saying that man's efforts alone will not get him into the Kingdom of God. Only God can save man and that is why he sent his only Son to Redeem Mankind!

V28   The disciples again are getting anxious and Peter speaks telling Jesus that they have nothing. They have given everything to follow him.

V29-31   Here Jesus is saying that whatever you give to God in Love, no matter how great or small your gift may be, you will be repaid one hundred times over. "When you give to the poor, it is like lending to the Lord, and the Lord will pay you back." (Proverbs 19: 17.) How great is God's generosity!

Jesus always speaks the truth and tells us very straight, that those who follow him will have to endure 'suffering' as it is part of our purifying process. It is a part of our spiritual growth.

Every individual has the opportunity no matter who they are, what they are, what they have done, past or present, to develop and attain spiritual growth if they so desire.

Man has the free-will to make the choice. Remember how Jesus speaks about the *'Servant'*, the one who will serve.

Jesus Speaks a Third Time about His Death

V32-34   They are now walking along the road towards Jerusalem. Notice Jesus is walking in front of them, well aware of what is going to happen when he reaches Jerusalem! He speaks to them in great detail about his death because he wants them to be prepared. This in fact is the third time that he speaks of the

Passion. As we will see, the disciples cannot possibly have taken in what Jesus is saying. Why? Was it because they just cannot bring themselves to accept that they are going to lose someone they love, 'so they turn a deaf ear'? Or is it that they truly do not understand? Revise Chapter 9: V30.

The Request of James and John

V35-37 As I said earlier they have not taken in what Jesus is telling them about His Death! It seems unbelieveable but it is true. They are preoccupied with a question that they are going to put to Jesus. They want to know if they can sit on either side of His throne?

V38   The cup and the baptism here means suffering.

V39   Jesus gives them a prophecy and tells them "You will indeed drink the cup..." for they both suffer. James is Martyred by Herod Agrippa, (Acts 12: 1) and then John suffers great persecution, but it is said that he is saved from death.

V40   Jesus tells them that they do not understand what they are asking! Jesus himself is to sit at the right hand side of His Father. He tells them that God has already prepared places for those who will enter His Kingdom.

V41   The other disciples show anger. So Jesus is going to give them another lesson.

V42   He gathers them around him. He explains to them that the pagan people have rulers and leaders that have complete power and authority over them, and they are held in 'awe' by the ordinary people.

V43-44 But this is not the way that you will live! He reminds them that to be 'great' in the Kingdom of God they must 'die to self' and become servants and serve their God on Earth. They must be humble and serve mankind with the words of God.

V45   He reminds them of the prophecy of Isaiah who speaks of the Messiah who will come as a 'Suffering Servant' to save mankind.

Jesus is the Messiah. Jesus is our example!

Jesus Heals Blind Bartimaeus

V46   They come to the city of Jericho, also known as the city of palm trees, but as Jesus is leaving for his long, hard walk to Jerusalem he comes upon a blind beggar by the roadside.

V47   The beggar calls out 'Jesus, Son of David!' This is very interesting because it is the first time, other than Peter, when someone calls him the *Messiah*. To the Jews the *Messiah* would be a descendant of King David, so to say 'Son of David' meant *Messiah*.

V48-52 You can imagine how Jesus felt. He knows that this is his last journey before His Passion. Yet even at this stage he will not pass someone in need. The crowds who are following Jesus are rejecting this beggar. Do you see their lack of love for their neighbour? Jesus took pity on him and calls him to come to him. When he tells Jesus that he wants his sight back, Jesus heals him. This is a very interesting situation because Jesus says to him "Go, your faith has made you well." Jesus continues on his way, with the blind beggar following him. Notice that Jesus never asks him to keep the miracle quiet. Is this because Jesus is fully aware that he is walking towards His Passion and that the time has come for everything to come into the 'open?'

Questions Mark Chapter Ten

1. Give an account of what Jesus says about divorce and what he says about living together before marriage.
2. Write out the Ten Commandments and learn them.
3. Why did Jesus bless the children?
4. Give an account of the 'Rich Man.'
5. How do you grow spiritually?
6. Why does Jesus speak for a third time about His *Passion*?
7. What request do James and John make
8. How does Jesus reply to their request?
9. Give an account of the healing of Bartimaeus.

St. Mark Chapter Eleven

Holy Week The Triumphant Entry into Jerusalem

Palm Sunday

Here Mark takes us into the Ministry of Jesus in Jerusalem. The Gospel is coming towards its climax with the death and resurrection of Jesus. This is to be Jesus' last week on this earth. He is aware of the tremendous suffering that is awaiting him and he has prepared his disciples as to what is to happen to their beloved Messiah. Everything he has told them is going to take place. (Read 10: 33-34.)

Here we will see Jesus in his first major role as the *Messiah*. Many people will recognise him as such, but there will be those whose hearts are open only to the influence of Satan and they will perform his evil works!

V1   When they reach the Mount of Olives, two of the disciples go to obey his orders.

V2   Jesus tells them to go and bring a colt back to him. Notice the words "You will find a colt tied up that has never been ridden." This shows Jesus' knowledge! The animal is very special! It is going to take a special person on a special journey!

This fulfils the prophecy of Zachariah 9: 9.

"Look your King is coming to you! He comes triumphant and victorious, but humble, and riding on a donkey– on a colt, the foal of a donkey."

V3   "Tell him that the Master needs it." This is a very interesting sentence because it indicates that the man knows Jesus and is expecting someone to collect the colt. The man is obviously

ready to deliver when Jesus calls. Are you ready to do the will of Jesus when he calls?

V4-6 Here is another lesson for us! The disciples obey Jesus in every way, even to saying what he tells them to say. Now, when we come up against difficulties with people, do we have the right answers? Do we ask God in our daily conversation with him what we should say to our neighbour, when we find ourselves in a difficult situation? I myself have gone through this experience and I can truthfully say that when faced up against my neighbour I was lost for words. I prayed inwardly that he would take over and give the answer.

Within seconds the Holy Spirit poured words out of me that left my neighbour absolutely stunned and speechless!!

When I was in the room with my neighbour and the words started to flow, I was completely at ease with myself. After leaving the room I must confess I felt completely shattered! However, I knew that it was not me who had spoken, but God had spoken through me. He had answered my prayer and had come to my rescue. Needless to say, I praised and thanked Him all day long. It is something I shall never forget till the day I die! This is what God wants of us as his disciples to-day. We must hear His words, be obedient and speak His words.

V7-8 To throw their cloaks over the colt is a sign that they recognise that Jesus is claiming Kingship. (Read 2 Kings: 9: 13.) Others throw branches and cloaks for the colt to walk over.

V9 There is tremendous excitement, and the people are shouting from Psalm 118 26. "May God bless the one who comes in the name of the Lord."

V10 As you read earlier, the Jews expect the *Messiah* to be a descendent of King David. So they are recognising that Jesus is claiming Kingship.

V11 If Jesus is claiming to be an earthly King, he would have entered Jerusalem on a horse, which is a sign of war, but he comes on a colt, which is a sign of Peace.

He would also have gone straight into the city, taken Pilate by surprise and attacked King Herod. Jesus does none of these things. He goes straight to His Father's House and you would have thought that, then, everyone would realise who he is!

The Jews expect that their *Messiah* will give them an earthly

Kingdom and free them from the Romans. But Jesus is claiming to be a Spiritual King with a Spiritual Kingdom. The Jews fail to see His Greatness!

Jesus Curses The Fig Tree

Monday

V12   They have no doubt spent the night in Bethany with Jesus' friends, Martha, Mary and Lazarus. Jesus is now coming back into Jerusalem. It is very important to remember the humanity of Jesus. He enjoys being with his friends and now he is hungry.

V13-14 The fig tree is symbolic of the House of Israel. Now Jesus has spent three years going round Israel preaching and performing miracles. He has shown them the Royal Road to His Father's Kingdom, for he has brought the New Covenant and this tells them that man has to bear fruit!

Yet they have not listened, they are spiritually deaf and Spiritually blind. Now this is the only time that you see Jesus passing Judgment.

He must have felt utterly heartbroken! Only the day before they had shown recognition and welcomed him as the *Messiah.* God has given Israel plenty of time to change their ways and follow the teachings of Jesus. Yet so many have rejected his message, so Jesus says, "No one shall ever eat figs from you again." What Jesus is saying is that Israel had its chance, but they failed, so now they are finished! Remember that Jesus is not cursing the fig tree. This miracle and parable is only an illustration of the faithless Nation of Israel.

Jesus Goes to the Temple

V15-17 Now this is a very great occasion for the Jews. It is the first festival of three for which they have to attend. "All the men of your Nation are to come to worship the Lord three times a year at the one place of worship: At Passover, Harvest Festival, and the Festival of Shelters. Each man is to bring a gift as he is able, in proportion to the blessings that the Lord your

God has given him." (Deuteronomy 16: 16-17.) Now the previous day as the Peaceful Messiah, Jesus goes to the temple straight away. Notice the words in V11 "Looked round at everything."

It is as though he goes not only to speak to His Father but to see that His Father's House is in order.

The Religious leaders allow the Court of Gentiles to be used as a market for trading animals and exchanging foreign, pagan, money. In this way they make a great profit for the temple and the Jewish trader will also benefit financially. The money-changers obviously make a good profit when they exchange foreign money into the Temple coinage. Foreign money cannot be used because it has the face of a pagan marked on the coin i.e. Face of Caesar. Here we find discrimination because the market is only allowed to be held in the Court of the Gentiles, but in the eyes of Jesus this is a place of worship. In fact the reason why Jesus is so angry, is that all this trading should have taken place outside the Temple. Needless to say he is not impressed with the dishonesty within His Father's House, "a hideout for thieves"; God's Temple is not for buying and selling. It is for receiving and giving the gifts of God. It is a place of worship and reverence. Israel has lost its spiritual life and legalism has taken the place of sincere worship and prayer. Prayer is our spiritual food. As individuals, if you lose your Prayer Life, you will lose your Spiritual Life also. Is it not true that if you do not communicate with your family or friends either by speaking, visiting or going out with them, the relationship will die? It certainly will not grow! Remember that the Temple is your heart. It is a place of prayer, 'a living Temple' and not a 'den of thieves.' It is a place where God can enter and where your Spiritual Life will grow in the Love of God.

V18-19 After seeing what Jesus said and did the religious leaders, Pharisees and Scribes, just want him dead! Notice the crowds reaction for they are once again 'amazed.' Notice also that whenever Jesus comes into the presence of people there are only two responses.

1. To repent and become a disciple of Christ.
or
2. To reject Him and follow Satan.
How do we respond to his teachings?

The Lesson From The Fig Tree

V20-21 The next morning they pass the fig tree which has withered from its roots. It is symbolic in that Judaism is dead.
"The people of Israel are like a plant whose roots have dried up and which bears no fruit." (Hosea 10: 16.)

V22-25 Here Jesus gives his disciples a lesson in Faith. Although they have seen and experienced His Power and Authority, he is going to remind them. He tells them to believe and never doubt the Power and Authority of God. 'For with God nothing is impossible.'
He tells them to believe and trust that prayers will be answered. He tells them that whatever problems they have in their life with their neighbour, be it anger or bitterness, command it 'to go' and it will. "Ask and you will receive," but first you must believe! This lesson is also for you and me!

The Question about Jesus' Authority

Tuesday

V27 The religious leaders are absolutely outraged at Jesus because of what he has done and said in the Temple. He has challenged their authority!

V28 They meet Jesus as he comes into the Temple with this question because they want to trap him, but they still do not realise who they are dealing with!

V29 Jesus is Wisdom itself. He therefore turns their question around and asks them a question.

V30-32 Jesus' question is a very wise and skilful one because everyone believed that John the Baptist was a Prophet, therefore he came from God. The Pharisees and Scribes will not commit themselves to say "from man" because this would have angered the people and deep down they know from whom John has received Authority. However, they themselves have not repented and been baptised in the baptism of John.

This shows that they have refused God's message. They have in fact rebelled against the word of God. So if they say 'from God', they will be admitting to their own downfall and to the fact that Jesus' message and Power does come from God. Remember that John had been sent to prepare the way for Jesus. Now if they openly accept John they will have to openly accept Jesus!

Their reaction is one of arguments between themselves because their very own question has put them into a 'trap!'

V33   Jesus knows that their answer is a lie because he can see into their hearts and he is well aware of their thoughts! Therefore he will not give them an answer because he knows that they know the truth. He has also given them a second chance to repent but they have taken the second response (V18-19) and rejected it.

Questions Mark Chapter Eleven

1. Describe the entry into Jerusalem?
2. Why does Jesus choose to ride on a colt?
3. What does God want us to do when we come up against difficulties?
4. How do the people show that they recognise that Jesus is claiming Kingship?
5. What do the Jews expect from their Messiah?
6. How does Jesus show his humanity?
7. Relate and explain the story of the fig tree.
8. Explain why Jesus reacts the way he does when he goes into the Temple.
9. How do the religious leaders try to trap Jesus? How does Jesus answer them?

St. Mark Chapter Twelve

The Parable of the Tenants in the Vineyard
This is also an Allegory

V1   Man – God
Vineyard – Israel, God's People
Fence around it – Protected with the Law of Moses
Tenants – Religious Leaders of Israel.

V2   Harvest Time – Remember the Fig Tree?
Slave – A Prophet

V3-4 That is how they dealt with some of the Major Prophets.

V5   These are the Minor Prophets.

V6   God then sends Jesus. "Last of all" means that this is our last chance! That there is not going to be another chance!

V7   Jesus is telling them that he knows they have premeditated murder in their hearts. (11: 18.)

V8   Jesus tells them this before he dies. In telling them what they are going to do, he is actually giving them another chance to repent.

V9   Vineyard – Kingdom of God, Israel.
Others – Gentiles, He wants us to produce spiritual fruit which the Jews fail to do.

V10-11 Jesus asks them if they remember Psalm 118: 22-23. The religious leaders know their Scriptures well and they are well aware that the parable spoken by Jesus is against them. They know that the 'stone' meant the coming of the Messiah but still they refuse to repent. Their hearts are filled with anger and they reject him. The stone is Jesus. The stone comes down the mountain and crushes the idol. The idol represented the different Nations: (Read Daniel 2: 34-35, 44-45.) The stone or rock is our salvation. Therefore we must become part of that rock. For it is prophesied in Daniel that the stone will become a great mountain and cover the whole earth. This is symbolic of Christianity growing spiritually throughout the world. Better to repent and be spiritually part of the rock, so that on the day of our Judgement we will not be crushed!

V12 The Jewish leaders are infuriated with Jesus and walk away, to plot for another day!

The Question about Paying Taxes

The Political Question

V13 Some Pharisees and Herodians gather together in the hope that they will get Jesus to say something that will condemn him in the eyes of the people.

V14-17 This is their first attempt to trap Jesus. They ask him a Political Question which is extremely dangerous at the time. They also say that they know he teaches, "The truth about God's will for man." How can they say this when they are still unrepentant? Although they are polite in their question, deep down is pure sarcasm! They think that they have really trapped Jesus with their question but they are to find in every single question they put to him, they are to receive an answer that has 'Fantastic *Wisdom*.'

The Political Question as I said earlier is very dangerous because Israel is under the rule of the Romans. If Jesus tells them to pay the taxes to Caesar, they will accuse him of being a traitor to his people.

If Jesus says, "do not pay taxes", they will give him over to the authorities as a rebel.

The Answer. He tells them to bring a coin. They produce a coin, which means they are using Caesar's money, therefore they are under Caesar's authority. Notice that Jesus did not have a coin! Jesus is His Own Authority! He asks them whose portrait is on the coin and they answer, "The Emperor's." Jesus says "pay the Emperor what belongs to the Emperor." But he is saying here that there is something they are not paying; there is a higher authority than the Emperor's and is God. Therefore he says, "and pay God what belongs to God." On the coin is the Image of the Emperor and Jesus is saying that all men are made in the Image of God and therefore you must give yourself back to him. (Reference Genesis) They have their answer, recognise Human Authority but recognise *God's* Authority as well.

The Question about Rising from Death

The Doctrinal Question

V18-27 Here the Sadducees try to trap him with a Doctrinal Question. Remember, these people do not believe in the Resurrection, angels or spirits. They come to Jesus with their question and quote from the Law of Moses.

The Answer. Jesus listens and then replies, "How wrong you are! And do you know why? It is because you do not know the Scriptures or God's Power. For when the dead rise to life . . . " Notice the word 'when' not 'if'; Jesus has just stated a fact. He explains that people will not marry because they will not be one in the 'flesh', they will be in 'spirit.' In other words they will have spiritual bodies not a human body. Now these people are expected to have great knowledge about the Book of Moses. The Book of Moses is the first five books of the Bible called the *Pentateuch*, which the Jews call the Book of Moses or the *Torah*, the *Law*. Now the Sadducees live strictly to the Law of Moses and their question to Jesus is a quotation from Moses. If Jesus disagrees with the Law of Moses, they will be very happy, because they will then have a reason to condemn Jesus. He says to them that he will explain something about the Resurrection because 'you do not know your Scripture. Have you not read about Moses and the 'burning bush'? Abraham, Isaac and Jacob have been dead over 400 years when God speaks to Moses. Jesus reminds them of what God says to Moses *"I Am"* in the *Present Tense*, "the God of Abraham, Isaac and Jacob", which means they are *Alive*. (Read Exodus 3: 2-6.) They are physically dead but spiritually they are alive.

Therefore God is the God of the living. Jesus is not only giving

TO LOVE GOD
IS TO LOVE YOUR NEIGHBOUR

Be a loving Mother, Father, Son or Daughter, Friend or Neighbour

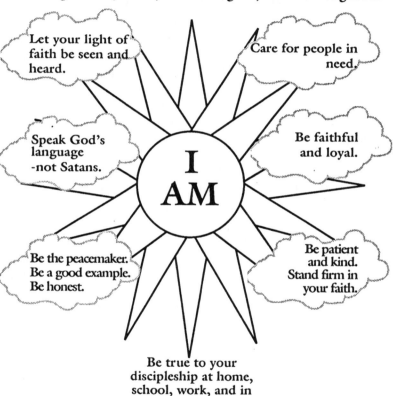

Let your light of faith be seen and heard.

Care for people in need.

Speak God's language -not Satans.

I AM

Be faithful and loyal.

Be the peacemaker. Be a good example. Be honest.

Be patient and kind. Stand firm in your faith.

Be true to your discipleship at home, school, work, and in your leisure time.

You are in charge of your own soul.
DO GOD'S WILL AND PRAY

them a lesson on the facts and conditions of the *Resurrection* but also *us*! Later we are to see by the power of God the *Resurrection of Jesus Himself.* This must have been of tremendous comfort for the believers at that time, as it is for all Christians of this day. Jesus finishes with a sharp sentence telling them how wrong they are!

The Great Commandment

The Moral Question

V28   The Scribes are determined to trap Jesus and so one of them put this question to him. Now the Jews have just over 600 Laws, some were Moral Laws, others were Ceremonial Laws. They are actually asking Jesus if he claims to know God's word so well, can he answer them in a sentence! Jesus does just that!

V29-31 **Answer.** Notice the number of '*All's.*' For with God it is *All* or *Nothing*! You cannot serve two Masters! Jesus answers them using the words of the Shema. Read Old Testament: (Deuteronomy 6: 4-6.) It is the daily prayer of every Jew and it begins with, "Listen, Israel! The Lord our God is the only God . . ."

V31 ′   He then links this by quoting from the Old Testament (Leviticus 19: 18.) "Love your neighbour as you love yourself." Now to the Jew, his neighbour would only be another Jew, certainly not a Gentile! So here is Jesus explaining their own Laws, yet they are still spiritually blind and spiritually deaf. You and I know who is our neighbour, irrespective of race, colour or creed. Indeed we would have 'Heaven on Earth' if everyone kept to these two Laws. If you truly loved God and your neighbour, you would not steal, murder or hurt anyone in any way! How well do you keep these Commandments?

V32-33 There is one Scribe among the people who calls out and says that Jesus is right. That the two Commandments Jesus has spoken of are far more important than any of the other Laws.

V34   Jesus says to him, "You are not far from the Kingdom of God." Jesus uses the words, "not far" because the man had obviously listened and understood the wisdom of Jesus' words. But still he has to repent and be baptised to enter the Kingdom of God.

There are no more questions because the Wisdom and Knowledge of Jesus is far too great for them.

You would have thought that they would have rejoiced at such Wisdom, but their hearts are hard and they went away in order to find other ways of 'Trapping Him!'

The Question about the Messiah

V35 David is looked upon as the Greatest King of Israel, God's anointed King, and the author of most of the Psalms. The Jews believe that the Messiah will be a descendant of David. Only partly the truth, for Joseph who married Mary, the Mother of Jesus, is a descendant of King David. In actual fact Jesus is claiming to be David's Lord. So he puts a question to them.

V36 This means that the 'Psalms' are inspired by the Holy Spirit and David himself states this. So Jesus quotes from Psalm 110: 1. "The Lord said to my Lord . . ."

V37 Now David calls him 'Lord.' So how can he be his Son? Therefore Jesus is saying that the only Son of His Father has to be someone with far 'greater power and authority' than David. Thus Jesus is claiming that 'power and authority' which is given to Him by God.

Therefore Jesus is claiming *Messiahship*. Many of the people are enjoying the teaching of Jesus.

Jesus Warns against the Teachers of the Law

V38-40 Here Jesus warns the ordinary people against the Scribes. The Scribes are well educated, know their Scripture and should have known everything about their religion. However, Jesus knows what is in their hearts and openly discloses their faults to the people:-

1 Love of show - 'Long Robes.'
2 Love of popularity - 'Greeted.'
3 Love of importance - 'Reserved Seats.'

4 Love of feeling superior - 'Best Places at feasts.'

5 Love of power-greed - 'Widows' Property', Consulted as Lawyer-charged high fees.

6 Love of pretence-hypocrisy - 'Long Prayers.'

Notice how much they 'loved' themselves, Jesus did! No wonder they do not want to change!

It would have been so uncomfortable to lose the 'love' of this kind of religious image! Yet because of this they reject the Greatest Love that Man has ever been given, they reject Jesus, their King and Saviour! In rejecting the teachings of Jesus they reject their own *Salvation*. For those who embrace the teachings and divine Love of Jesus, they will be accepted into Everlasting Life and the Love of God.

The Widow's Offering

V41   Jesus watches what is given in terms of self-sacrifice. He is sitting by the treasury and people would put their offerings into a chest as they leave the Temple.

V42   The Widow quietly put in her two coins. The rich people draw attention to themselves when they put in larger amounts.

V43   Jesus tells his disciples that the Widow gave far more than any other person in the Temple. Because it is not what she gave, but the spirit in which she gave it is of far greater importance.

V44   The Widow gave everything she had! The others gave what they could spare.

Questions Mark Chapter Twelve

1. Give an account of 'The Tenants in the Vineyard' and explain its meaning.
2. Give an account of the Political Question and the answer Jesus gave.
3. Give an account of the Doctrinal Question and the answer Jesus gave.
4. Give an account of the Moral Question and the answer Jesus gave.
5. Why does Jesus say to the man "You are not far from the Kingdom of God?"
6. What warnings does Jesus give to the people?
7. What does Jesus say about the Widow's offering?

St. Mark Chapter Thirteen

The Destruction of the Temple

When you are reading this chapter, I think that it is very important to note some of the words that Jesus uses frequently.
'Be on guard', V5, V9, V23, V35. Jesus is saying 'listen and do what I tell you.' But some people do not listen!
'Do not worry' V11. You do not have to worry if you believe and your Faith is strong.
'Pray', V18: Watch, V33, V34, V37. Jesus is saying be ready and do not be taken unawares by anything.
In this chapter Jesus prophesied about the destruction of the Temple in Jerusalem and the *Second Coming*! He tells the people about it well before His Passion and Death, but many do not listen.

V1-2 This Temple is built by King Herod the Great. He has the Temple built in the hope that it will make him more popular with the Jews. It is never fully completed for it took forty-six years to build the part that Jesus teaches in.
Herod is certainly not great spiritually, in fact he is a very immoral man as we read earlier. As they leave the Temple one of the disciples looked back in admiration of it. You can imagine how he must have felt when Jesus tells him that it will be destroyed!

Troubles and Persecutions

V3 Interesting to note that Jesus is sitting on the Mount of Olives, because it is from here that he Ascends into Heaven. Notice that whenever Jesus is faced with something of great impor-

tance Peter, James and John are usually there with him.

V4   Notice how they put their question. They do not ask why. They have learnt that when Jesus speaks and says that something will happen they know it will, and they want to be ready.

V5   Jesus warns them about being deceived, for that was his great concern for them He does not mention when or where disaster will come.

V6   Notice the word 'many.' Is it not true that many strange man-made congregations have sprung up over the years?

V7-8 I know that this has been the history of man from the beginning. However, over the last few years man is aware of what the Atomic Bomb can do! More countries have been at war with one another. There is great dispute and fighting in countries throughout the world over political, religious or racial prejudice. There have been more earthquakes than has ever been recorded before and I am sure that we are all aware of the terrible famines in the third world. It is all happening to-day. So did you take note of the First Warning in V5- do not let anyone lead you away from the Word of God.

V9   Here comes the Second Warning. Jesus has told his disciples that great suffering awaits him and that those who follow him and teach the 'Good News' will also suffer. Paul bore witness to what Jesus is saying here. You can read in the Acts of Apostles how Paul underwent everything Jesus mentions. The early Christians suffer great persecution especially under Nero who has Peter crucified. Peter chooses to be crucified upside down. Many others suffer death because of their faith in Jesus.

V10   Since the time of Jesus, Christianity has spread throughout the whole world. Yet there are people who are still spiritually deaf and spiritually blind.

V11   The persecution of the early Christians is only the beginning. It has gone on throughout the centuries up to the present day. Many Christians are being persecuted at this very moment in various parts of the world because of their Faith. e.g. 'San Salvador.'

However Jesus tells us not to worry, we will be given the strength and the words to bear our oppression.

V12   We know that this happened in Germany in the last war within the German Youth. Some exposed their parents who did not believe in Nazism. There were families who betrayed each other in Russia and suffered greatly at the hands of Communism.

V13   He asks us to keep faith and stand firm when we come up against oppression. We have to be His witnesses on this earth and this means letting people see that God is the most important person in our life. Therefore we must keep his Commandments and live as he asks us to live, a life of love, for God and our neighbour.

People will reject or laugh at you when you refuse to do something that you know is wrong in the eyes of Jesus. Remember that even Jesus is 'tried and tested' and so we will also be 'tried and tested' by people of no faith or little faith. Jesus has told us this; he has hidden nothing from us because he is the '*Truth!*' As you grow in Faith, just like the early Christians, you will suffer, but Jesus will be by your side all the time. 'He is only a prayer away!' Better to walk away from evil, even to lose those you think are 'friends', than to lose your soul! Better to pass the test Jesus has set, hard though it may be, than to fail and lose an Eternal Life of Love with him. Heaven awaits all who are willing to follow Him into Eternity.

The Awful Horror

V14   'The Awful Horror' is described in the Book of Daniel 9:27 as a 'pagan image'. It is also mentioned in Daniel 11:31 and 12:11.

You must understand that the 'Holy of Holies' is the most sacred part of the Temple to the Jew. It is so sacred, that the High Priest is only allowed to enter this room once a year.

Here he speaks the name "Yahweh", which means Father, then withdraws from the room. The Jewish people believe that the presence of God is within the 'Holy of Holies.' Now, what is this 'Awful Horror'? In AD70 the Jewish people rebel against the Romans but are defeated. The Roman Emperor and his army enter the Temple and go into the 'Holy of Holies'. Here they erect the standard of the Roman Legion which has an eagle on its banner. You can just imagine the 'horror' in the hearts of the Jewish people. To them it is obviously a most profane desecration of their Temple. The Temple is destroyed. It has taken forty-six years to build but is never fully completed. The only part that still exists to-day is the 'Wailing Wall.' Following the rebellion, the disciples and followers of Jesus are persecuted. You can read about this in the Acts of Apostles. Then comes the destruction of the City when it is set on fire.

V15   Many Christians flee out of Jerusalem before the final attack.

V16-20 Jesus' prophecy here is not just about the destruction of Jerusalem. He is speaking about a most deadly devastation that will come on all mankind.

He has intermixed the destruction of Jerusalem with the prophecy about the end of the world. Jesus tells us that the suffering at the end of the world will be so horrific, that it will be unequalled by anything that man has ever had to contend with before! Verse nineteen is mentioned in the Old Testament. (Daniel 12: 1.) But God has shortened the time of horror so that people will survive. Great destruction will occur before the end.

V21-23 Here Jesus is warning us not to believe people from man-made sects who say that they come in his name. It is a Solemn Warning! (Read Deuteronomy 12: 32: 13: 1-4.) ..."Do not let anyone deceive you with foolish words...." (Ephesians 5: 6.)

The Coming of the Son of Man

V24-26 Here Jesus tells us about His Second Coming. Note that there are only two comings of God to Man!

The first time he came in Mercy. He came to give man the chance to repent and be baptised in the Spirit. He brought forgiveness and healing. He offered the New Covenant to all men.

His second coming will be in Judgement. It will be, so the Scriptures tell us, so horrific that some people will die of fear. People do not like this part of Scripture and tend to put it behind them. What has been described here will happen, for all prophecies are fulfilled. The world is living in such terrible wickedness that something will have to happen to bring man back to his senses! Look back in Exodus to when the Jews lived in slavery and injustice for nearly 400 years. It is not until they are so sick of suffering that they cry out to God to come to their aid. God is only waiting for them to 'ask' and when they do, He answers their prayers. Are we praying with our whole hearts 'asking' for God to come and heal us? Good and Evil cannot live together. Jesus said, '*I am the Way, the Truth and the Life,*' and he gave us all free will to choose to accept or reject him. Therefore when he comes, as he will, he will judge all mankind as to how they have lived out the 'Word of God.' Pray that we will all stand firm in the Love and Light of Jesus within our Lives.

V27 For those who have lived according to his words it will be a fantastic time, especially if they are still alive when he comes. But for those who deliberately rejected him there will be incredible fear!

The Lesson of the Fig-Tree

V28 Remember the story of the 'Fig tree' in 11: 13-14. The Fig tree is the symbol of the House of Israel and the Summer is the Harvest. Here Jesus tells us that 'Summer is near.'
Now in 1948 Israel began to blossom, after 2000 years of barrenness and after being told by their Messiah, "Israel, God's hand is on you now in Judgement." Israel is literally withered and the people are scattered over the whole world. They have no country of their own, but in 1948 the Jews, after great suffering return to their homeland Israel. Jesus is telling us that through History we will see when the 'Harvest is Near' and that means 'His Second Coming!'

V29 The Jews of Jesus' generation, as we have seen, are unbelieving Jews. However Paul says in Romans 8: 29-30. "Those whom God had already chosen he also set apart to become like His Son, so that the Son would be the first among many brothers .... and those he called, he put right with himself and he shared his Glory with them." (Read Romans 9, 10, 11.) Jesus is saying that towards the end, Jews will be converted and reconciled with God. It is then that Jesus will be seen in his 'Second Coming.'

V30   Jesus is promising that this will come true. All God's prophesies are fulfilled because he is the *Truth*.

V31   The words of God are immortal.

No One Knows the Day or Hour

V32   Only God himself knows the time of His Second Coming.

V33-37 Count the number of times he uses the word 'watch.' He is giving us a solemn warning to be ready for His coming. When Jesus refers to the word being 'asleep', he does not mean 'physically.' He wants all men to be ready 'spiritually' and be well prepared to receive him. We should ask ourselves that if he came at this very moment would the Temple within us be fit for God to enter? 'Being asleep' means allowing ourselves to drift away from the way God wants us to live. 'Being awake' means that your faith is active and alive.

Has the temple within you had 'a spring clean'? faith grown in your lives and are you living according to the Laws of the Love of God?

Questions Mark Chapter Thirteen

1.   What does Jesus say about the Temple?
2.   Give an account of the first warnings that Jesus gives to his disciples.
3.   Give an account of the second set of warnings that Jesus gave.
4.   What is "The Awful Horror"?
5.   What does Jesus tell us about His Second Coming?
6.   What does Jesus mean when he says 'stay awake', 'be alert' or 'watch?'

St. Mark Chapter Fourteen

The Plot Against Jesus

Wednesday

V1   The Passover festival is celebrated once a year. It is very important to the Jewish people because it is to commemorate how God takes his people out of the land of slavery in Egypt, into the promised land. They have celebrated it since the time of Moses. The name comes from when the Angel of Death 'Passed Over' their homes. (Read: Exodus 12: 12-14.) All Jewish males are expected to make the pilgrimage to the Temple in Jerusalem. Here they will offer a young lamb in sacrifice, as a form of thanksgiving. Then they will eat the lamb at the Passover meal. This will include eating unleavened bread which is a symbol of the women in the time of Moses hastily making bread for their journey. They have no time to put yeast into it to make it rise, therefore it is 'unleavened.' They will also eat bitter herbs to remind them that once they were ill treated slaves! During the meal they will drink wine and pray. The story of Moses leading his people, by the Power of God, out of Egypt is always told by someone in the group. In this way the story of the Passover is passed down from one generation to another into every Jewish family right up to the present day.

The Pharisees and Scribes are plotting a trap for Jesus, for they want him dead.

V2   Obviously they do not want to arrest Jesus during the time of the Passover, because they are frightened that the followers of Jesus will cause a riot . They may well have considered that Jesus would gain more support if the 'teachers of the Law' disrupted their religious festival.

Jesus Is Anointed at Bethany

V3-5 Jesus goes to Bethany to the home of Simon the Leper. Note the words, 'had suffered' which implies that Jesus had cured him. A woman comes forward and pours an expensive ointment over Jesus, which signifies that she is showing great reverence to him. Many of the people consider it to be a great waste.

It cost 300 denari. To earn this amount of money will have taken about 300 days of hard work. In the Gospel of St. John we are told that Judas is one of the people who objected.

V6-9 Normally a King is anointed before his coronation and also people before they are buried. The Jews look towards their Messiah as the 'Anointed One' of God. No wonder Jesus says, "She has done a fine and beautiful thing for me." For here is Jesus in Wednesday of Holy Week, just before the night of his tremendous agony and fully aware that he is going to face a most grotesque and horrific death! He accepts this woman's act of love in anointing his body before he dies, with the honour that is due to him as the Messiah, the King of Kings. He tells his disciples that they also should see to the bodies of God's children as did this woman, which is a great act of mercy. When they show their anger towards her, Jesus tells them that the world will always be full of poor people. (Read: Deuteronomy 15: 11.)

He reminds them not to neglect the other works of *Mercy*. What Jesus is saying is that the 'Body of Christ' is the 'Church' and the jar of expensive perfume is the 'gift' that God has given to his people to pour over the 'Body of Christ.'

Therefore we must always love and honour 'the body of Christ', which is the Church.

We are the Church of Christ and the Holy Spirit lives in us. We must therefore use these gifts to serve God and our neighbour. The woman uses the gift of love when she anoints Jesus.

Judas Agrees to Betray Jesus

V10-11 Here we have one of Jesus' close friends going to betray his master for thirty pieces of silver. Why? Is it that Judas thinks that Jesus will be an earthly King, crush the Romans and rule with great power? Many Jews expect this of the Messiah. When Jesus enters Jerusalem and goes straight to the Temple, is Judas disappointed even then? Does he think Jesus will go straight into the city and claim his Kingship? Is it that Judas hoped to obtain a high position when, as perhaps he thinks, Jesus will rule? John's Gospel tells us how angry Judas is when this woman anoints Jesus in preparation for his death. Jesus has warned his disciples about his suffering and death. Is Judas spiritually deaf to the words of Jesus and is the act of this woman the final turning point for Judas?

We only know that he does accept money in return for information as to the whereabouts of Jesus that night. The Chief Priests do not want to take Jesus during the day because it would have caused a great disturbance with the people, or even a riot. As Jewish men are dressed the same it requires Judas to point Jesus out during the night. However I do not think that Judas expects to see Jesus treated in the way he is, for the taking of his own life suggests great remorse.

Jesus Eats the Passover Meal with His Disciples

Thursday

V12 Remember the *Passover* is to commemorate the Jews' deliverance from slavery. The lamb to be sacrificed is to be a male lamb without spot or blemish. On the following day, *Friday*, the 'Lamb of God,' a male lamb, literally without spot or blemish, will be sacrificed on Mount Calvary at the very moment that the Jews sacrifice their male lambs in the Temple. This is to be the Greatest Passover that ever took place.

Jesus is going to pass over from Death to Life.

We are going to pass over from Judaism to Christianity.
We are going to pass over from sin to forgiveness.
We are going to pass over from evil to goodness.
We are going to pass over from darkness to light.

V13   A very interesting sentence and a good sign for the disciples, because only the women carry the jars of water.

V14-16 Remember in Chapter 11 when Jesus sent the disciples for the colt, the owner is expecting them. Here again you have the same situation. The owner of the house is waiting for them but the disciples do not realise it. God has provided for His Son's journey and for the last meal with his disciples.

V17-18 Judas is sitting at the table when Jesus speaks these words. Psalm 55: 12 says, "If it were an enemy that mocked me, I could endure it...." Jesus must have felt very sad looking into the heart of Judas and seeing his weakness. Psalm 55: 13 says, "But it is you, my companion, my colleague and close friend..." The prophecy is fulfilled.

V19   They are shocked by what Jesus has just said. The eleven at least seem to be searching their hearts; "not me!" they are saying.

V20   At that very moment Judas is dipping into the same dish as Jesus, so they all know. "The one who shared my food, has turned against me." (Psalm 41: 9.) In John's Gospel we are told that Jesus tells Judas that whatever he has to do he must go and do it quickly. At this point Judas leaves them.

V21   It is recorded that Jesus will die in the Old Testament Scriptures. Isaiah 53 gives such a detailed prophecy of the *Passion* that you would think you were actually present.

In Isaiah 53: 10 it says, "The Lord says, it was my will that he should suffer; his death was a sacrifice to bring forgiveness." Jesus is obviously prepared to carry out His Father's will. Even up to the very last moment Jesus leaves the way open for Judas to repent.

The Lord's Supper

V22   Judas has left so he never knows the significance of the Death of Jesus. It is here with his faithful eleven disciples that Jesus

gives them the last and greatest lesson of all. He institutes the Blessed Eucharist towards the end of the Passover meal. He takes the bread and breaks it saying, 'this is my body.' This meant that his physical body will be broken on Calvary. He is introducing them to the awesome mystery of how he is going to feed *His Church* for all time.

V23-24 As was said earlier, a covenant is an agreement between two persons. One person is God and the other person is man. Now Jesus is here instituting the greatest covenant of all time with man. Remember that a Covenant always has a sign. The sign is Jesus' own blood. He takes the cup and says, "This is my blood which is poured out for many." Every time the host and cup are lifted up, we should remember that Jesus gave his Body and Blood, willingly, so that man could be saved.

Note The Words—

> He Took – All the sins of man upon himself.
> He Broke – He broke himself for us.
> He Gave – Himself as a gift.

He gave us the bread that we would always be fed with the presence of God and therefore we would be close to him. He asks us to remember that it is *His Covenant*.

I wonder when we see the *Host* and the *Cup* raised up do we realise the *Awesome Mystery* that we are confronting. Do we realise that we are actually in *His Presence*? Remember the High Priest could only enter the 'Holy of Holies' once a year for a very short time, because he was in the presence of God. Yet we can receive him every day of our lives. Do we really realise how incredible our privileges are today.

Jesus provides for his people. He gives us the Eucharist which is our Spiritual Food. It is Christ's Presence within us. He desires that we should show His Presence daily within our lives. That is to pour out to our family and neighbours, His Love, His Compassion, His Peace, His Joy, His Help, His Generosity. We should remember that we are the people of the "Book and the Bread" and live a life of Love.

V25 This is the wine on the table. The new wine is the Holy Spirit.

As soon as he steps out into Gethsemane, the Kingdom of God is already on the earth, but Jesus is going to pay a high price for it to happen.

Jesus has taught them the Commandments they must keep and the way they should live. He has shown them the way to Eternal Life in Heaven.

He tells them that he will not drink wine again until it is the Holy Spirit that is poured out. As soon as His Resurrection and Ascension takes place, he receives the Holy Spirit, the new wine. He then pours it out on the Church in *Pentecost*.

Pentecost starts on Whit Sunday. We keep this feast in memory of the Holy Spirit coming down on the apostles.

V26   They sang from the Psalms. So here, you have Jesus and the leaders of the Church singing the Psalms, so the Old Testament Scriptures are the word of God!

The Eucharist

Dear Father, I give you my hands to bless
That when I receive the Holy Eucharist,
Your Loving Grace will stay within
Making my life, my works, worthwhile for Him.
Take my hands, use them to do graceful deeds,
Where there is poverty, hunger, I will feed.
When I see loveless ones in great despair
I'll give them my heart, they will know you care.
My feet, you gave, I'll use to walk your way,
Then into your house I will come and pray.
I'll 'thank my Father for all He has done
For He gave the life of His own dear Son,
That man could escape a sinful nightmare
Of having to live within Satan's Snare.
Your words, my Father, I will always heed,
In love I'll teach to those who live in need.
Dear Father, your works I'll do where I can
For life without you, Lord, is just a sham!

Jesus Predicts Peter's Denial

V27   The quotation Jesus uses from the Scriptures is from Zachariah 13: 7. He is using this prophecy to show them that he knows that they will desert him, but he understands their weakness. This occurs before the Resurrection and before Pentecost.

V28   Here he tells them that after the Resurrection he will meet them in Galilee. The first message that they will get on Resurrection day will be.. "Go and meet me there."

V29   Peter is the first to say that he will never desert Jesus even if the others do.

V30   Jesus tells Peter exactly what he will do. There must have been great sadness in Peter's heart because he does love Jesus.

V31   Peter protests and says that he would rather die. You will notice that Peter is the spokesman for the others and they always agree with what he says.

Right from this situation and after the Resurrection and Ascension takes place, Peter's leadership is unquestioned and he is the one who makes all the decisions.

Jesus Prays in Gethsemane

V32   Jesus is about to face one of the most terrible moments of his life. In this time of great anguish he turns to His Father in prayer. He does what we should all do in times of distress and that is *Pray*.

V33   He takes Peter, James and John with him. They have witnessed His *Transfiguration* on Mount Hermon and now he wants them present during his great agony and humiliation in the Garden of Gethsemane. When Jesus goes into Gethsemane a most incredible '*Spiritual Warfare*' between *Good* and *Evil*, between *Heaven* and *Hell* is going to start.

When people are in trouble or distress it is good to have close friends around you to share your problems. Jesus also needs to know that his friends are close by.

V34   Many people think that the greatest suffering that Jesus went through is being nailed to the cross.

This is not so. It is in the Garden of Gethsemane that we see the humanity and the awesome agony that Jesus goes through which nearly killed him. He is well aware that he has to make a decision. He is also aware that millions of people will never even thank him for giving His Life for them. This causes tremendous sorrow within His Heart.

He asks the disciples to stay awake and he means this both spiritually and physically.

V35   There is such an agonising battle going on inside Jesus that he 'prostrates himself before God.' This means that he falls flat on the ground and prays. Luke tells us that his agony is so great that he perspires 'blood.' Jesus asks if there is any other way out of this suffering. He cannot at this moment face it. It is very necessary to be aware of the humanity as well as the Divinity of Jesus. In his suffering he faced the powers of *Hell* alone and he did it for all mankind. He did it for you and me!

V36   He calls, "My Father. Take this cup of suffering away from me". Jesus asks to be taken out of this horrific, agonising situation. Within the darkness there is absolute silence. God's silence is saying that this is the only way, that only Jesus can carry the cross to save mankind. Jesus understands the silence and the love behind it. He knows God wants His Son to fulfil His perfect will for him on earth. Jesus has gone through a most horrendous battle, but in the darkness of sorrow and suffering says, "Yet not what I want, but what you want."

V37   Jesus returns to his disciples for he is in great need of comfort from his friends. There are no loving words of comfort or support because they are asleep. He calls to Peter, who one day is going to be the leader of the Church on earth. Jesus says to him, "Simon are you asleep?" Remember in Chapter 13 how Jesus has warned his disciples to 'stay awake', 'watch', 'be alert' and here he finds them, at this most critical moment in his life, fast asleep. The physical sleep is not the problem but spiritually they are not alert. They have no idea what is going on. They certainly do not realise that the decision Jesus has to make meant whether they would be saved or not!

I think had they realised, they would have been down on their knees praying with him!

Are we 'spiritually alert'? Do we truly realise what the eternal consequences will be unless we live up to the Laws that Jesus taught?

There is a great warning for us here and it comes under the words, "one hour". Jesus is explaining that a 'Spiritual Warfare' is going on and that if difficulty is found in staying 'awake' spiritually for one hour, what will happen throughout our whole life? Once you become linked with Jesus, you are in a 'Spiritual Battle' and have you not already found that to be true? Satan will do everything he can to prevent you from growing spiritually and getting closer to God. He does not want you to go, after death, where he can never go! That is, to an eternal, glorious life in Heaven with Jesus. You will find that your friends will try to prevent you from following the way of Jesus. They will even walk away from you and other things will happen that may well hurt you because you have chosen to be one with God. As Jesus has to make a great decision to save mankind, so too will we be faced with the decision to follow Jesus and serve him; or follow Satan and do his evil works on this earth.

V38   He tells them to stay awake and pray that they will not be tempted. Notice Peter sleeps for one hour before he is put to the test and what happens to this man who sincerely told Jesus that he would die before he would deny him; he fails the test! "The spirit is willing but the flesh is weak."

V39   Jesus goes back again to stand up against the temptations and evils of Satan. What did he do? He prayed to God to help him overcome this awesome agony. This is what we must also do when faced with anything that is not of God, *Pray*. God will hear our prayers and He will come to our aid.

V40   Again he goes to pray and once more he returns to find them asleep. They cannot find words to excuse themselves.

V41   The third time he returns they are asleep again. But this time it is all over. Jesus has fought the 'Spiritual Battle Alone.' He has made the decision to do His Father's will without any support from them. He has gone through tremendous agony to save mankind and they have not even stood by his side.
The final hour of Redemption has begun.

V42   Jesus has warned them many times to 'stay awake' or 'be alert', but he meant this in the spiritual sense. He is concerned

about them being 'spiritually asleep' not 'physically asleep.'
Otherwise he would not say 'Get up, let us go.'

We can appreciate his concern, for we are going to see
the disciples 'spiritually asleep' or almost, throughout the
crucifixion. They are going to be absolutely bewildered and
demented with suffering because they do not listen when he
tries to prepare them for the events to come. They are not
'spiritually awake.' If they had been, they would understand
the three prophecies about the *Passion* the fact that he has to
die. They should have been of comfort and support to him
during his awesome agony.

Jesus actually goes out to meet his betrayer. This is very important, because Jesus makes a voluntary sacrifice of His Life,
it is not taken from him.

The Agony in the Garden

You knelt upon your Fathers earth,
No star no light, as at Thy birth,
Darkness covered Gethsemane
For here you chose to die for me.
You called upon your Father's name
Yet not for power, yet not for fame,
"Thy will be done", Thy humble call,
You died within to save us all.
Devoured by jealousy and spite
They came upopn you in the night,
They took upon themselves to try
SON of GOD, Son of the most HIGH.
Oh lonely night, Oh lonely heart,
Unworthy man did play his part.

The Arrest of Jesus

V43   Here is a warning for us! Judas, one of his closest disciples,
turns against him and betrays him.

V44-46 Because it is late and therefore dark, Judas commits a most
incredible insult. He goes up to Jesus, so as to point him out in
the dark and kisses him. A kiss is the usual greeting of

affection but Judas uses it as a sign of betrayal. The words "Take him away under guard" is absolutely absurd. Obviously Judas never really knew Jesus, because if Jesus had not wanted to go, he could easily have made himself unavailable!

V47   John's Gospel tells us that this is Peter who is trying to defend Jesus. Peter understands physical battles but he has yet to learn through the *Passion* and *Resurrection* the meaning of 'Spiritual Battles.' Do we understand that hatred, jealousy, bitterness and anger are Spiritual Battles that we must fight against, otherwise they will destroy us. When are we going to understand the real meaning of *God's Love, Love for our Neighbour.*

It is then that we will be able to stand together as one in Christ and fight all the evils of Satan and his followers in this world!

V48-49 Jesus tells them that there is no reason for swords and clubs. He has made his decision and he will go with them of his own free will. He is going to fulfil the Scriptures. They must have been astounded at his reaction!

V50   Again you see the fulfilment of the Scriptures when the disciples run off.

"All of us were like sheep that were lost, each of us going his own way. But the Lord made the punishment fall on him, the punishment all of us deserved."

(Isaiah 53: 6.)

Later these men will give their lives for Jesus, but at this very moment they are spiritually weak.

V51-52 Some people think that this is Mark who comes to warn Jesus, but there is no factual evidence that it is. Whoever he is, when he sees what is happening he also runs away!

I think they run away not just because they are frightened, but because they are under considerable shock. They just cannot believe or comprehend why this has happened to Jesus, their great and powerful leader, their Messiah!

Jesus before the Council

V53   Jesus is taken before the Supreme Court of Israel.

V54   Peter follows at a distance, though he is no doubt still shocked

V55   They can find no evidence against him.

and bewildered. There must have been love in his heart, for he wants to know what is happening to Jesus.

V55   They can find no evidence against him.

V56   Because the witnesses' stories do not agree, the trial should have been stopped. One of the many reasons why it is illegal in the first place!

V57   They lie against Jesus. Note that it is late at night and it is against their own rules to hold a trial at night. So you have the Sanhedrin meeting illegally to pass a death sentence on someone they know is innocent.

The evidence does not really matter to them, for they already have premeditated murder in their hearts. They are frightened of Jesus and they are prepared to break their rules, tell lies, do anything to get Jesus sentenced to death.

V58-59 Here Jesus is referring to His Resurrection. Judaism is finished and when he rises on the third day there will be a New Covenant, a new life. Those who accept Jesus will have the Temple of God within them.

V60-61 Jesus would not reply to the lies of these witnesses because Jesus is the *Truth* and no *Truth* is spoken. He does answer the second question because it is the *Truth!*

V62   Jesus answers, "I am." Remember God said this to Moses and it means the Past, Present, and Future. (Re-read 12: 18-27.) Jesus speaks on adding to His *Messianic* claim and gives them a prophecy. (Re-read 2: 28.) If you are sitting in the highest honour with God it means you are equal with him.

V63   The High Priest in anger at the answer Jesus gave tore his clothes. He cannot accept that Jesus is the Messiah and therefore charges him with blasphemy.

V64   They brought in a verdict of guilty and that he should die. Two years later we see the fulfilment of Jesus' prophecy (V.62) when Stephen is falsely tried by the very same Sanhedrin. Stephen said, "I see heaven opened and the Son of Man standing at the right-hand side of God." (Acts 7: 56.) The fact that the Sanhedrin could not see is due to their own spiritual blindness!

V65   Jesus is condemned. Try and imagine how Jesus must have felt. The people for whom he is going to willingly give his life are spitting at him and treating him "as if he were nothing." Isaiah 53: 3. He is humiliated and rejected.

Peter Denies Jesus

V66-72 Peter is still spiritually asleep. He is still bewildered by these events and he shows that he suffers from the 'fear of man.' We see this when he is confronted with the fact that he is a follower of Jesus. He denies this even to the point of saying that he never even knew this man. So here we see Peter frightened to death of having his name linked with Jesus, because he fears what the people might do to him. However when the cock crows a third time Peter breaks down and weeps.

He remembers the words of Jesus. If we read Acts 5: 1-11. we will find a very different Peter. Jesus has to heal Peter of the 'fear of man' and start living with the 'fear of God', which means fear of losing God's Love.

After being baptised and filled with the Holy Spirit, the Power of God, and as leader of the Church, Peter is well able to fulfil whatever Jesus asks of him. Here in the Acts we find him fulfilling God's word by exposing the sin of Ananias and his wife Sapphira. Peter climbs high up on the 'Spiritual Mountain' and even his shadow heals the sick. Peter fulfils his mission and the Church grows in numbers and in Holiness. So here we see how the 'weak' Peter is transformed into a 'rock.'

Jesus wants to transform all of us away from the 'fear of man.' Do not be afraid of people laughing at you, criticising you, or rejecting you. Better to accept all the insults and to live in the Love of God, so that one day like Peter you will share God's eternal Glory!

Questions Mark Chapter Fourteen

1. Explain the Passover Festival.
2. Why do you think Jesus accepts the anointing?
3. Why do you think Judas betrays Jesus?
4. Give an account of the Passover meal.
5. What is a covenant?
6. Give an account of the Lord's Supper.
7. What does Jesus say to Peter? What is his reaction?
8. Give an account of what happens in the Garden of Gethsemane.
9. Why do the disciples run away?
10. Give an account of Jesus before the Sanhedrin.
11. What does the 'fear of man' mean?
What does the 'fear of God' mean?
12. What finally happens to Peter?

St. Mark Chapter Fifteen

Jesus is Brought before Pilate

Friday

V1   Although the Sanhedrin have condemned Jesus to death they have to obey the Roman rule. This means that they have to have it confirmed by the Roman Governor, who at this time is Pilate. Notice that it is early in the morning, about 6 a.m., for this is the time when it is legal to hold such a trial. Notice the words "had their plans ready." This tells us that they fully intend to kill Jesus whether it is right or wrong. Even so, they have a plan to tell Pilate that Jesus is claiming to be 'King of the Jews.' The stress was on the word "King" so that such a claim will be seen as treason against the Roman State!

But where has Jesus been between 12 O'clock and 6 a.m.? The evidence seems to be that after they condemn him, late Thursday night, he is then put into a solitary cell. The cell is two floors underneath the ground and he is in total darkness. Underneath the Priest's house is a prison where the Apostles are kept and flogged. It is still there to this day.

Underneath this cell is the solitary cell where they put Jesus. It only has a very small window, which does not allow any light to get through. So Jesus spent those six hours without light, water or company, after being spat at and beaten by the guards. This is the fulfilment of Psalm 88: which you should read.

V2   Pilate questions Jesus and asks him if he is a King? Jesus is far too clever and he says to Pilate, "So you say".

V3   They make many accusations against him.

V4   Pilate asks him to speak up against these accusations.

V5   Jesus will not answer to the lies of these men. He finds that the correct answer to lies is silence. *Truth* speaks for itself!

Jesus is Sentenced to Death

V6-14   It is the custom at *Passover* for the Roman Governor to release a prisoner whom the people name. A man called Barabbas is imprisoned at this time. Now this in fact is one of the most symbolic events that happen at the crucifixion. Barabbas is a murderer, a thief and a Zealot.

He is therefore an enemy of the Romans. He has committed all the crimes that Jesus has been accused of and is going to be put to death for these crimes.

The word **Bar** means 'the son of' and **Abba** means 'father.' Therefore the name Barabbas means, 'the son of his father.' Pilate offers to let Jesus go free, but the Chief Priests have moved the people into an irrational and ungovernable mood. They demand the release of Barabbas and the crucifixion of Jesus. Even Pilate knows that Jesus is innocent and that Barabbas is full of guilt. Barrabas represents you and me. He deserves to die but is set free, so that Jesus can take his place and die to save mankind.

So now we have *Infinite Goodness* taking the place of evil.

The Scourging at the Pillar

They tied your gentle hands up high,
A sorrowing heart did breathe a sigh.
Whips that scourged caused mortal distress,
Bleeding cuts amassed Holy Flesh.
How could man's heart be evoked
To draw Thy blood with evil stroke?
No seed of love within had grown,
Their hearts were just like white washed stone.
Oh gentle heart, sweet love divine
That echoed words that "You are mine".
Oh lonely night, oh lonely heart,
Unworthy man did play his part.

V15   This is a very important verse. Read it carefully! Pilate signs the death sentence to calm the crowds and to please them! So the Gospel evidence shows us that Jesus is put to death for

committing absolutely no crime at all. He is utterly and completely innocent.

Jesus is taken, tied to a pillar and whipped. Many prisoners actually die under this punishment. Jesus must be physically strong to endure such horrific agony. The Roman whips have small spikes of metal attached and they dig into the back, tearing away at the flesh. Jesus must have lost a great deal of blood.

Crowning with Thorns

It was no game they played that day
Our Saviour dear was made to pay.
For salvations sake HE did bear
Man's sins, grown in satan's snare.
They placed and pushed upon HIS head
A crown of thorns, sweet tears shed.
For blood and sweat poured down Thy face
Borne only for the human race.
Our sins indeed were pain enough
Without mockery and rebuff.
Dear Lord have pity on us all,
Give us the grace to hear your call.
Oh lonely night, Oh lonely heart,
Unworthy man did play his part.

V16-20 The soldiers allow people to watch while they taunt him. This game they play with Jesus is called 'the game of Kings.' You will find evidence of it on the flagstones of the *Praetorium* in Israel. You see the soldiers worship the Emperor as a God. When they find themselves governing other countries like Israel, they play this game of dressing up an effigy as a King. This is symbolic of the people's representative and they mock the effigy and eventually burn it in front of the people. Yet in the case of Jesus, they play their game of incredible mockery with a human being! Now the Jewish people are watching all that is going on and yet they do not realise that the soldiers are making a mockery of the whole Jewish Nation! Their brutality and inhumanity towards Jesus is incredible.

This is one of the most horrific parts of the *Passion*, which should not take place. A normal crucifixion does not contain a scourging!
"We ignored him as if he were nothing."
Isaiah 53: 3.
They crowned him with thorns. This is symbolic of the laurel wreath worn by Emperors and they think it is a great joke. First they put a cap on his head and then beat the thorns into his head. There is very clear evidence for the fact that Jesus is dying on the road to Calvary. He must have lost a great amount of blood through all this cruelty. The crowning and the scourging is enough to kill any man!

Jesus Is Crucified

V21   Simon of Cyrene represents *All of Us*. However Jesus will not 'force' us to carry the cross, we have free will, and we must choose. We are no longer in the position of Barabbas the sinner unwilling to take the cross. Jesus has made it possible for us to take up His Cross willingly and walk with him in our lives and eventually into *Eternity*.

V22   Golgotha which means 'The Place of The Skull' is very symbolic of the Wisdom of Man! They took their King, their Saviour, their God to this place to put him to death. Does this not show the *Emptiness* of *Man's Wisdom*?

V23   He refused this drug.

V24   It is also prophesied that they will cast lots for His clothes. (Psalm 22: 18.) Then they *crucify Him*.
"He was treated harshly, but endured it humbly; he never
said a word. Like a lamb about to be slaughtered, like a
sheep about to be sheared, he never said a word."
Isaiah 53: 7.

V25   They crucify Jesus at the Third Hour—9.00 a.m.
The Sixth Hour—12 Noon.
The Ninth Hour—3.00 p.m.
At 9.00 a.m. the Jews kill the male lamb to be offered in sacrifice. As this is happening God's pure *Lamb* is being sacrificed on *Calvary*. So the real *Passover* is taking place here and the *Christian Passover has Begun*.

V26   When a crucifixion takes place, they put each man's crime over his head. This is to let the public see why they have been put to death. Above the head of Jesus they put a sign "The King of the Jews." Sometimes above a cross you will see the letters I.N.R.I. This is short for the Latin 'Iesus Nazarenus Rex Iudaeorum', which means "Jesus of Nazareth the King of the Jews."

V27-28 Two other men are crucified one on each side of Jesus. This fulfils the prophecy of Isaiah 53: 12. "He willingly gave his life and shared the fate of evil men."

V29-30 The people mock Jesus and this fulfils the prophecy of Isaiah 53: 3. They are still totally spiritually blind, and fail to realise that Jesus is on the cross for them!

V31-32 The Chief Priests taunt him, "Come down from the cross now and we will believe;" Remember Thomas, he wants proof that Jesus has risen from the dead.

        Jesus does say that if people fail to believe in the Scriptures, they will not believe in the Ressurection.

        As Christians we have the Bible. We have the word of God speaking to us and we know that Jesus rose from the dead. Therefore we have no excuse at all to live any other way than the way he taught us!

The Death of Jesus

V33   From 12 noon until 3.00 p.m. the whole country is covered in darkness.

V34   At 3.00 p.m. Jesus cries out in his own language, Aramaic, "Eloi, Eloi, lema sabachthani" which is the first line from Psalm 22. This cry of Jesus comes from the very depth of His heart and he sees himself as "a worm despised and scorned by everyone!" (Psalm 22: 6.)

        His cry is also one of respect and reverence to God who seemed far away. "O Lord, do not stay away from me!" (Psalm 22: 19.) "Praise him, you servants of the Lord!" (Psalm 22: 23.) Jesus is crying out for God's presence! This fulfils the prophecy of Psalm 22.

        The most intolerable thing of all is not to have God's presence. *Hell* means to be separated from *Love, Life,* and *Light.* Remember we make the *Choice* for ourselves!

V35   They misunderstand the words of Jesus.

V36   Someone put sour wine to the lips of Jesus but we do not know
       who. Further we do not really know why. Is it someone who
       feels for Jesus in his agony or is it someone who wants to keep
       him alive to see if any great miracle will occur?
       Some of the people watching do not feel anything at what they
       are witnessing. Others feel terrible and some even repent and
       believe.

V37   Before Jesus dies, he gives a 'Loud Cry.' This is one of the
       most fantastic things that happened. Jesus has lost most of His
       Blood and the fluid in His Body. Therefore it is from a medical
       point of view, completely impossible for him to do this. But
       because he is truly the Son of God, his last breath breathed a
       great Cry of Victory!
       For he has conquered *Satan* and saved mankind from *Eternal
       Death*. He descended to *Satan* and took from him the keys of
       death and *Hell*.

       "I am the first and the last,
       I am the living one! I was dead, but now I
       am alive for ever and ever, I have authority
       over death and the world of the dead."
       Revelations 1: 18.

       So Jesus conquered our four greatest enemies *Sickness, Sin,
       Death* and *Hell*.
       A crucifixion is one of the cruellest ways of dying. It is a slow
       death and the record time is known to be seven days. The
       normal time for a man to last on a cross is about three days.
       You died from thirst, exposure and the inability to force
       yourself up to breathe; you died of suffocation. Jesus has been
       through such excruiating brutality that by the time they go to
       see if he is dead, there is only a trickle of blood and then
       water. Most of his blood has been spilled into the earth. On
       Calvary, which is the Roman name for Golgotha, Jesus' blood
       went into the earth and it cries out for redemption and
       mercy.

V38   As Jesus dies the curtain covering the 'Holy of Holies' is
       destroyed. This symbolises the end of Judaism.

V39   The Roman soldier has been greatly moved by what he has witnessed. Although an unbeliever at first he is transformed. This must be true, because he speaks the truth and is no longer spiritually blind. Unlike the religious leaders and others, he recognises that, "This man was really the Son of God."
"But he endured the suffering that should have been ours, the pain that we should have borne."
(Isaiah 53: 4)

V40-41 It is interesting to note that the women who follow Jesus stay extremely faithful to him. Women have no legal rights and are very much 'sinned against.' Jesus is certainly revolutionary in their cause and on many occasions defends them. Also Jesus accepts the ministry of women as seen in Luke 8: 2-3. Jesus is anointed by a woman before his death. Jesus has his feet washed by the tears of a woman.
Women go to the tomb to anoint the body of Jesus. After his death it is a woman whom Jesus first appears to. At Golgotha it is the women who stay. Notice that Scriptures tell us that the women help him in Galilee. Also that "many other women" had followed him to Jerusalem. It is not accepted that women should go about on their own, but yet they risk their lives and all they have, to be disciples of Jesus. It is stated that he has 72 disciples but we do not know how many are women. In the Acts of the Apostles at the beginning, Acts 1: 14 you find the women carrying on the work of Jesus by the side of the men. The men however abandon Jesus after he is arrested. Only Peter and John stay at a distance to see what is going on.

My Lord

They nailed my saviour to a tree
High on a hill on Calvary.
Such bitter pain did he endure
That man could walk through heaven's door.
Man gazed upon a broken heart,
Body beaten, pain that did smart.
Blood and tears welled upon thy face,
Tears of anguish for the human race.
The heart of Jesus ravaged by

the sin of man, the baby's cry.
A gift from God, a loving seed
So hungry for the love it needs.
Monstrous man who rejected Him
In preference for a life of sin.
Your wanton greed brought bloody war
Killing young and old by the score.
Hunger, poverty did exist
For satan's snare you couldn't resist.
His power evolved within your heart.
In life your neighbour played no part.
Oh King of Love, Oh King divine,
We are the branches, You the vine.
Come forth and bless our everyday
That we may walk the Royal way.
Oh Saviour dear, so filled with pain,
you died that we would live again.
Oh lonely night, Oh lonely heart,
Unworthy man did play his part.

The Burial of Jesus

V42   It is the day before the Sabbath and according to Jewish custom it is shameful to have crucified men still hanging on the cross on their Holy Day. Normally these men would be left on the cross for their bodies to rot. They are never buried, for their bodies are given to the wild animals to devour. It is most exceptional that both Herod and Pilate allow the body of Jesus to be taken away to be buried.

Joseph of Arimathea is a Prince and a very wealthy man. He is obviously a very good man and he put his reputation at great risk by going and asking for the body of Jesus. He is, like Nicodemus, a member of the Sanhedrin and no doubt this act would displease many because he associates himself with Jesus.

V43   However, 'Joseph went boldly.' In other words, even though his reputation is at risk, he is convinced that his request is the right thing to do. He wants the body of Jesus to be buried in his family tomb. By this very act he is telling Pilate that he believes Jesus to be innocent and worthy of a proper burial.

This must make Pilate feel very uncomfortable, for he also knows that Jesus is innocent but he has signed the death sentence due to 'fear of man.'

V44   Pilate's first reaction on hearing that Jesus is dead is one of surprise. To hear that he has died within hours, when it normally took about three days, is hard for Pilate and others to believe. He therefore ordered a test to be carried out. A lance is put into the base of the heart, so that if he is not dead it will kill him immediately. Pilate does the Christians a great favour by ordering this test to be carried out.

   If proved beyond doubt that Jesus is dead, when he rises from the dead, no one can possibly say it is a 'trick.'

V45   Only the criminals have their legs broken, so as to hasten their death, for it prevents them from heaving themselves up to breathe.

V46   Joseph of Arimathea's family tomb is a cave that has been cut into the rock and prepared to take the bodies of his family. This is spiritually significant because Jesus is the Rock of our Salvation and His Body is laid on pure rock.

   "The stone which the builders rejected as worthless turned out to be the most important of all."
(Psalm 118: 22.)

V47   The women are there watching right up until the end. They see that he dies and that he is buried in a tomb which is sealed by a large stone. Had Jesus still been alive when taken down from the cross, he would have died of suffocation inside the tomb. The evidence from the Scriptures most certainly show that Jesus died on the cross.

Questions Mark Chapter Fifteen

1. Why do you think that the religious leaders want Jesus dead?
2. Give an account of the 'crowning with thorns' and the 'scourging at the pillar.'
3. Give an account of the 'Crucifixion.'
4. Who is greatly touched by the death of Jesus?
5. Why does Jesus have to die?
6. Give an account of the burial of Jesus.
7. What part do the women play as followers of Jesus?

St. Mark Chapter Sixteen

Resurrection

Easter Sunday

There are two endings to this chapter. The first one is between V1-8, and then a whole new ending between V9-20. Mark's Gospel ends abruptly in verse 8. We do not know the reason for this but someone completed his work. The second ending is a summary of what is said in the other Gospels.

V1   Notice it is the women who go back to the tomb with spices for they want to anoint the body of Jesus. They have to wait until the Sabbath is over before they can visit the tomb. So now we are into Sunday which we call Easter Sunday.

V2-4   As they go on their way they start to discuss how they will get into the tomb. It is not until then that they have realised that it will be completely impossible for them to remove the huge stone that seals the entrance. When they arrive they see that the stone has been removed.

V5   They enter to find a young man dressed in white. The reaction of the women is one of alarm or they are filled with 'amazement.' Whenever a miracle occurs, remember the people are 'amazed.' This person, man or angel, is obviously a messenger from God.

V6   All four Gospels say, 'do not be afraid or alarmed' and this is the first message that Jesus gives to his disciples. He does not want them to be frightened because he knows that they are looking for him and they expect to find his body in the tomb. They are told that he is not to be found among the dead, "God is the God of the living." Remember Jesus told the Sadducees

this because they did not believe in the Resurrection (12: 18.) Therefore anyone who comes in search of Jesus should not be frightened because He has *Risen*, He is not among the dead, He is among the living.

V7　They are told to go and give his disciples a message and notice it says 'including Peter.' Jesus does not want Peter to think that the message was not for him . Peter may well have thought this because of his denying Jesus. It has left him in great sorrow for acting the way he did. So here we see God's great love and compassion, not only for Peter, but also for the other disciples who abandoned him.

Jesus wants to meet them in Galilee because it represents the world. Galilee is the place of the Gentiles and Jesus started his Public Ministry here. From here Jesus wants his ministry to go world wide.

V8　The women run away because they are frightened and do not speak of the event to anyone. This is the first ending of Mark.

Jesus Appears To Mary Magdalene

V9-11　To show himself firstly to Mary Magdalene who is a sinner, is of great importance and meaning. He has to die to save sinners, but he rises again in Victory of 'Life over death.' This is a message for all sinners and Mary Magdalene is there representing all of us! The Resurrection is the greatest message for all of mankind!

Mary goes and tells the others but they do not believe her.
The Lord says, "It was my will that he should suffer; his death was a sacrifice to bring forgiveness."
(Isaiah 53: 10.)

Jesus Appears to Two Disciples

V12-13　Jesus appears as a traveller to two of his disciples. They go and tell the others but again they will not believe it. It is not that they do not want to believe, it just seemed 'too good to be true.' They really miss Jesus and they dearly want him back

with them. They are still grieving about their conduct towards him. They are full of guilt and sorrow for having deserted him. They are so greatly burdened with their guilt that when told he has come back, they just cannot take it in. Within their hearts they know he is the only one who can heal them and take away their guilt; but it is too much to expect.

Jesus Appears to the Eleven

V14   Can you imagine the reaction of the disciples when he appears before them! He tells them off for their lack of Faith, because they did not believe those who had seen him after he had risen. Jesus prophesied it three times before he died. He told them that the Scriptures would be fulfilled. Throughout all this they realise that Jesus is really present with them.

They are obviously overjoyed even though they are being reprimanded for their disbelief. The one thing that makes Jesus happy is when people believe, but when people do not believe it makes him very unhappy. He has chosen them to be the leaders of His Church and he never wants them to disbelieve ever again!

V15   The Great Commission that is given is to "go" out into the whole world and proclaim the Good News to all men.

V16   To enter the Kingdom of God you must be Baptised. It is understood that you cannot be condemned, unless the message of God has been preached to you and you have made the choice to accept or reject it!

If you reject God's message, the Scriptures say very clearly that you have put yourself outside of *Salvation*.

V17   Believers must be identified with Jesus. Believers are the 'branches of the Vine' and like the sap that runs through the Vine, we must let God's grace pour into our lives. Then we will be able to do his work on this earth.

V18   This has happened to many missionaries in the Far East where there was no serum to cure them after being bitten by snakes. They just prayed and asked God to cure them and they were cured.

If I have the right to pray in the name of Jesus that a person will be healed, either spiritually, physically, or even both

according to the will of God, I should really ask myself, am I really and truly identified with Jesus, because then I can use *His Name*!

Jesus Is Taken up to Heaven

V19-20 Here Jesus takes his place of *Honour* on the right hand side of *His Father*. It is here that he can intercede for us. This is one movement of the Church.

The second movement is the Church spreading throughout the world with Jesus present. Even though He is in Heaven, He is working with the Church on earth.

When the word of God is preached the people will be set free. When they have repented, the Lord will work inside of them. Always be ready for the second coming of Jesus.

Repent – Turn away from all evil.

Believe – Let Jesus show you how to live.

Receive – Accept the gifts and graces He gives you and use them for the greater Glory of God.

Go – Live in the Love of God, not in the 'fear of man' and spread his word.

Stay Awake – He will come when you do not expect him!

The Measure

Do not measure me my, friend, by what I give
For God alone did give me one life to live,
Hidden deep within my very self unseen
He's there, no matter what I do, to redeem.
Thus, when kindly words are spoken or deeds done
It is not I, but the Grace of God, The Son.
'Tis truth indeed when we speak to him in prayer
Of our needs, for he'll not leave us in despair,
For God is love, and all pain He'll take away
When sorrows come, joys will fill another day.
So, my friend, just measure me in His grace,
Let us join together making Christ our base,
In love let us do His work upon this earth,
As Christians let us go showing men rebirth,

And where we find those under a savage strain
Let our hearts seek to comfort, and ease the pain;
And the suffering we find let us try to share
Remembering the Cross that He alone did bear,
Therefore, measure me in love, my Christian friend,
And from this true purpose, never let me bend.

Questions Mark Chapter Sixteen

1. Give an account of the Resurrection.
2. Why do you think Jesus appears to Mary Magdalene first?
3. What is the reaction of the disciples when Jesus appears to them?
4. What is the Great Commission that Jesus gave to his disciples?
5. What is required of us to enter into the Kingdom of God?

THE KINGDOM OF GOD

GOD LOVES YOU

GOD CHOSE YOU

"YOU ARE MINE"

God is infinite love, mercy, goodness and generousity.
Jesus lives in my heart, and I will grow in his love.

SEED OF THE KINGDOM

Nourish the seed by receiving him, trusting
him and speaking to him.

Be a true disciple of the King...Live by his word.

And the seed of the Kingdom within you will
grow into...

Love, joy, peace,
patience, kindness,
goodness, faithful-
ness, humility and
self control

Bring heaven on earth
"Do God's will"
Communicate with God and neigbour

The Kingdom of God

What do we find in this Jesus who walked the earth over 2,000 years ago? We find infinite *Love*, infinite *Compassion*, infinite *Generosity*, infinite *Wisdom*, infinite *Mercy* and so on. Everything about Jesus is infinitely *Good*. He is the *Christ Incarnate*. So here we have just a glimpse of the Kingdom of God.

The Kingdom means the spiritual reign of God and he sent Jesus to establish this into the hearts of men on earth.

When Jesus comes into this world it is covered with a cloud of evil. Israel literally is a wilderness, but once you have Jesus coming on earth, you have light (God's power) coming into darkness (evil) (John 1: 5).

If *Goodness* is coming to replace *Evil* then man has to change. He has to repent and be baptised. When Jesus comes out of the waters of Baptism, though he is without sin, he brings a new creation. (Mk. 1: 10).

Jesus speaks about the Kingdom in the present and in the future. When he tells them, in the present, that the Kingdom "is near" (Mk. 1: 5), we accept that the Kingdom of God is standing right in front of them in the person of Jesus the Christ. At that moment they fail to recognise this because they are spiritually blind.

When Jesus speaks in parables about the Kingdom he uses images which people can understand and to which they can relate. In the parable of the Sower Jesus speaks about the Kingdom in the future. Here Jesus is sowing the Word of God in men's hearts, later he will reap the harvest, (Mk. 4: 1- 9). This parable is also an examination of conscience and a call to remain steadfast in one's faith. In Mk. 4: 26 Jesus teaches about what the Kingdom is like. Here we have a parable of hidden growth. Jesus can see into the hearts of men and he knows the response to his word.

The parable of the Mustard Seed (Mk. 4: 30) again illustrates the growth of the Kingdom. It is such a very small seed but so, too, is Jesus' group of twelve followers. However, the mustard seed will grow rapidly into a large bush and so too will the Kingdom of God. Christianity is to spread rapidly through the whole world.

Jesus in his teaching makes reference to the children around him. He says that, "the Kingdom of God belongs to such as these" (Mk. 10: 14). He sees the innocence and sincerity of the children and he is saying that a child's attitude to its mother and father is one of total love. A child puts all its security and trust into the hands of its parents. Therefore so must man respond to his *Father* in Heaven if he wishes to enter the Kingdom. "I assure you that whoever does not receive the Kingdom of God like a child will not enter it" (Mk. 10: 15). Jesus warns man that he must receive the Kingdom as a child receives a gift, with deep gratitude and humility. No one can ever earn the Kingdom because it has been offered as a gift by God.

Jesus reveals that, when anyone puts all their security in wealth and not in God, they will find it difficult to "enter the Kingdom of God" (Mk. 10: 25). He instructs the people that the two most important commandments are *Love God* and *Love your Neighbour*. When one of the teachers of the law agrees with Jesus, Jesus says to him "You are not far from the Kingdom of God" (Mk. 12: 34). This man like everyone else has first to repent and be baptised before he can enter into God's family. To have the Kingdom of God within ourselves we must have absolute love and desire to follow the teachings of Jesus. We must live his word and become *Christlike* in our thoughts, our words and in our actions. The *Kingdom* of *God* is everything that is *Good*. It is *Perfect Love, Kindness, Generosity, Joy, Goodness, Mercy, Peace* and *Compassion*.

Is it not true to say that if everyone behaved in this way we would indeed have *Heaven* on earth. To achieve this we must do *God's will*! *He* wants nothing but the *Best* for all *His children*. When you want to accomplish something in life, you have to follow the rules. A footballer trains, a dancer trains, an actor trains, an athlete trains, a singer trains, and they keep the rules. They may well find it hard, but they have to discipline themselves in order to achieve their *Goal*. Reach your *Goal* by keeping *God's Rules*!

In his teachings of the future Jesus warns man to be ready for the final coming of the Kingdom of God, the end of time. "No-one knows, however, when that day or hour will come" (Mk. 13: 32).

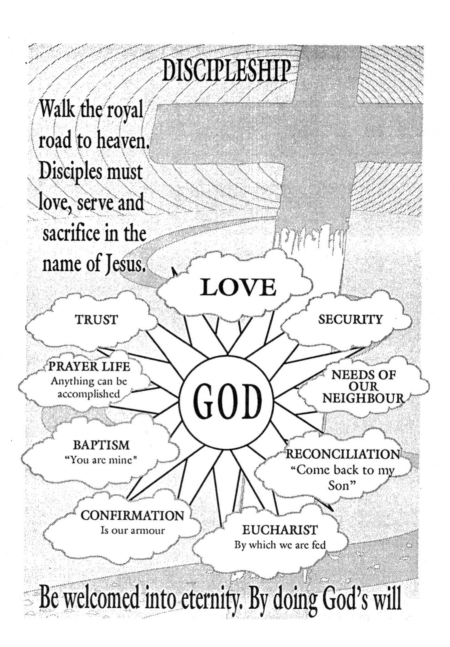

Jesus has clearly given us the formula to enter the Kingdom of God, and make preparation for eternal life. This we call heaven. The bridegroom invites us all to his banquet in Heaven and we can either accept or reject the invitation. We make that choice here and now!

"You will see the Son of Man seated on the right of the Almighty and coming with the clouds of heaven" (Mk. 14: 62).

Discipleship

The word *disciple* comes from the Latin word *discipulus* which means *learner*. Today we understand the word *disciple* to mean a follower of *Jesus the Christ*. Jesus comes on earth to establish the reign of God in men's hearts and to free them from the slavery of sin. Jesus is a wise teacher, a master teacher and he knows that he will require faithful and obedient men to help him. He chooses twelve apostles and apostle means 'messenger.' The number twelve here represents the twelve tribes of Israel. However the apostles are going to go out into a *New Israel*, for Jesus has brought a *New Covenant* and they are to preach the *Good News*.

"Come with me and I will teach you to catch men" (Mk. 1: 17). This is the message for all the twelve. They will learn from their Master teacher. They will see him show his power and authority, perform miracles and cast out evil. They will hear his profound teachings and they will be called to follow his example.

Among the twelve are fishermen, a tax collector and a zealot. Having a tax collector and a zealot living, working and praying together is an excellent example of 'love for one's neighbour'. They did of course have divine love living amongst them, together with a supreme personality and a sense of divine direction. Is this the reason why they dropped everything and followed him?

In his teachings, Jesus clearly explains that a disciple is one who "does what God wants him to do" (Mk. 3: 35). He further explains that a disciple can have any role within God's family, as long as you put the word of God into action.

In Mk. 6: 7-13 we see some of the qualities that are displayed by the twelve as they set out on their missionary work. Their mission will face rejection or acceptance. They will certainly have to rely on the love of a neighbour, for they set out with totally nothing but the word of God in their hearts. They must have had tremendous faith, courage, patience, dedication, obedience, love and loyalty (except for one) to fulfil this mission for Jesus. Jesus gives them the authority to go and preach, drive out demons, anoint the sick, heal the sick and they obeyed without question.

Discipleship in the world today still maintains these same principals. Christianity still continues in the battle against injustice, hunger, the homeless and the sick. All these and many more 'shelter under the branches' of Christianity. Following Jesus' declaration of his suffering and death, he says, "If anyone wants to come with me he must forget self, carry his cross and follow me . . . . (Mk. 8: 34-38). In other words, if you want to be a disciple and gain eternal life, (which is God's gift to us), then it will cost a great deal. A true disciple will be called to walk the same road as Jesus and follow his example.

It may well involve suffering and rejection, especially in today's society. Indeed some may well be called to die for their faith.

Disciples will be called to *Love, Serve* and *Sacrifice*. We see that the very first action of the apostles is one of *Sacrifice*, for they leave their families, their work and everything that they owned to follow Jesus. Religious today make this very same self-sacrifice. When we take up our cross, we accept all our faults and failings and give ourselves completely to God. He will then bless us and use our lives for the glory of His Kingdom. "Everyone will be purified by fire as a sacrifice is purified by salt" (Mk. 9: 49). This means that we will be purified through suffering, but purification is a never ending process within our lives.

In Mk. 9: 33-38 we find the disciples in a human situation. "Who, was the greatest?" Jesus can read their hearts and explains that to be great one must live a life of service "Even the Son of Man did not come to be served, he came to serve and to give his life to redeem many people" (Mk. 10: 45) said Jesus. In addition Jesus tells the disciples that greatness lies in a child's attitude, for it puts all its trust, love and security into the hands of its parents. Therefore a disciple must indulge in this attitude towards God and serve humbly.

When James and John make their request to sit on his right and left hand in the Kingdom (Mk. 10: 35-45) they do not realise what they are asking. Jesus himself is said to be sitting on the right hand of His Father, They appear not to fully understand the Spiritual Kingdom of God, but are thinking in terms of a worldly kingdom. "Come and follow me", (Mk. 10: 21) says Jesus to the rich young man who wants to know how he can achieve eternal life. He fails the test that Jesus put to him, because all his security is in worldly wealth.

True discipleship, true greatness is following the example of Jesus the Christ. True discipleship can be found in the act of the widow's offering. "She gave all she had to live on" (Mk.12: 44). Jesus measures this act as one of self-sacrifice.

To be a true follower of Jesus may result in your being rejected by your friends, or even your family. Rejection is a very painful process. However if we walk with Jesus, we follow in his footsteps. Discipleship is very costly, but remember that Heaven is priceless! In his great love for mankind, Jesus has given man the strength to walk the royal road. This strength is obtained through the Sacraments.

When we receive the Sacrament of Confirmation, like the apostles, we are given the power of the Holy Spirit to witness for Christ. (Acts 1: and 2:). This Sacrament makes us mature and responsible Christians within the Church. We should take notice of Jesus' words, "Go throughout the whole world and preach the Gospel to all mankind" (Mk. 16: 15). No matter what our vocation is in this life this message is for you and me. He wants us to live by the word and put it into action. He asks us to reach out within our family, our friends, our neighbours, in our workplace and by our example of being *Christlike*, bring others into His *Kingdom*. To help love grow between yourself, family and friends, communication plays a very important part. When we fail to communicate, love and friendship fade or die. Our prayer life therefore is of great importance and must be taken seriously. We must keep the 'line open' with God for 'through prayer anything can be accomplished' (Mk. 9: 29). To love God, to love your neighbour and to live according to *His Word* is surely the essence of *Discipleship*.

"Since Christ is our peace, we shall be living up to the name of Christian if, by letting peace reign in our hearts, we let Christ be seen in our lives"

St. Gregory of Nyssa.

A Christian

I wonder why God chose you,
  To do his work on earth,
  Your heart explains the answer,
  You offer men re-birth.
  Searching deep into the soul,
  Seeing the stress and strain,
  You seek only to comfort,
  To cherish and sustain.
  Hope and trust within the Lord,
  God's peace is your refrain,
  Gentleness in you is found,
  Sweet grace do you retrain.
  For Christ-like is your image,
  Sweet gift of love you bear,
  Thus sufferings that abound you
  You take yourself to share.
  Amidst toil and confusion,
  Loneliness and dismay,
  Through a dark and bitter world
  You bring light on my day.
  I can lean on your shoulder,
  I can weep by your side,
  Because you are a Christian
  And God in you abides.

Jesus in Mark's Gospel

Mark introduces Jesus right at the beginning of his Gospel as the Son of God, the *Christ*. *Christ* is *Christos* in Greek, the word *Messiah* is Hebrew and they both mean the *Anointed One*. The Jews have once been a great people in the days of King David and King Solomon. They believe that a *Messiah* will come and be the *Anointed One*, a descendant of King David. He will be both a political and religious

JESUS IN MARK'S GOSPEL

Son Of Man ⟶   ⟵ Son Of David

SON OF GOD

2:V10	10:V33
2:V28	10:V45
8:V31	13:V26
8:V38	14:V21
9:V9	14:V41
9:V12	14:V62
9:V31	

Old Testament

VISION DANIEL
7:V13-14
HOLY SERVANT
IS:V42 IS:53:V2

LORD 2:V28
MASTER 11:V3
BRIDEGROOM 2:V19
PREACHER 1:V38
TEACHER

1:V22	10:V17
14:V14	10:V20
4:V38	10:V51
5:V35	12:V14
9:V5	12:V19
9:V17	14:V45
9:V38	

OWN DEAR SON
12:V6
SON OF THE MOST HIGH GOD 5:V7
GOD'S HOLY MESSENGER 1:V21
PROPHET 6:V4, 8:V28
SON OF MARY 6:V3
JOHN THE BAPTIST
ELIJAH 8:V28
KING OF THE JEWS
15:V2,9,12,18,26,32
THE MESSIAH 8:V29

"You are my own dear son"
1:V11

"This is my own dear son"
9:V7

"This man was really the son of God" 15:V39

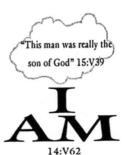
14:V62

"SON OF DAVID"

10:V47,48

Old Testament

"HE WILL RULE AS KING DAVID'S SUCCESSOR" IS:9V7

Old Testament

"THE NEW KING FROM THE ROYAL LINE OF DAVID WILL BE A SYMBOL TO THE NATIONS" IS11:V10

Old Testament

"SEE NOW YOUR KING COMES TO YOU" ZECH9:V9

figure who will free them from the slavery of Roman rule and make Israel the greatest nation on earth.

Mark is eventually going to unfold for us that Jesus is indeed the *Messiah*. The secret of Jesus' identity – *Messianic Secret* – has to be kept until he has completed his Father's mission. Now Jesus is the complete opposite to what the Jews expects of their *Messiah*. It is not until the Resurrection that an irrefutable claim can be made to *Messiahship*. Mark portrays Jesus in his Gospel as the Servant of God, "Behold my servant" (Isaiah 42: 1). You see Jesus in his humblest role, for this is the Gospel of the Worker. He has come as God's servant to do the work and will of his Father by establishing God's Kingdom on earth. When he emerges from the waters of baptism – though he has no sin – he brings a *New Covenant*, a *New People*, a *New Law of Love* and *Redemption* for man. His Father says, "You are my own dear Son, I am pleased with you" (Mk. 1: 9 - 11).

Let us look at some of the titles in Mark's Gospel in relation to Jesus.

In Mk. 1: 29 the word "straight" implies that Jesus goes immediately to Peter's house. One associates these words with that of a *Servant*. So here you see Jesus instantly obeying his Father's will. Notice that after Simon's mother-in-law is healed she gets up and waits on them (Mk. 1: 31). God expects disciples to serve and be active members of the Church. Throughout Mark's Gospel you see that Jesus chose to be God's Holy *Servant*. He sets the example for us all.

In Mk. 1: 38 Jesus says, "We must go on to the other villages round here. I have to preach in them also because that is why I came." Here we see Jesus as the *Preacher* going to spread the word of God to all men. It also reflects the image of a *Servant* fulfilling his *Master's* will.

This can also be found in Jesus' own words when he said that he had *"not come to be served, he came to serve" (Mk.10: 45).*

Again in the Garden of Gethsemane he said *"not what I want, but what you want"* (Mk. 14: 36).

Jesus refers to himself as *Lord* (Mk. 2: 28) and *Master* (Mk. 11: 3). Indeed Jesus is *Lord* and *Master* of all creation. Therefore the

Sabbath and the colt belong to him He can do anything he wants with them. The titles indicate one who requires service. "The Sabbath was made for the good of man" (Mk. 2: 27). Jesus wants man to serve him by keeping the Sabbath Holy. Jesus requires the service of a colt to take him into Jerusalem "The *Master* needs it" (Mk. 11: 3).

Jesus refers to himself as the *Bridegroom* (Mk. 2: 19-20) and the guests are his disciples. He wants them to enjoy themselves in his presence, because one day he will have to leave them to fulfil his Father's will. A *Bridegroom* at his wedding would certainly not want his guests to fast, rather would he want the guests to enjoy the banquet before he left. Jesus is illustrating the fact that He is the bridegroom of the New Israel and the disciples are His representatives.

When Jesus calls himself *Teacher* again we see in Mark that he requires service. "The *Teacher* says, where is the room where my disciples and I will eat the Passover meal?" (Mk. 14: 14).

The word *Teacher* is *Rabbi* in *Hebrew*. The people call Jesus *Teacher* and they are "amazed at the way he taught, for he wasn't like the teachers of the law, instead he taught with authority" (Mk. 1: 22). Indeed, he is the *Master Teacher* who uses simple words to get over a most profound message. He taught the message of Salvation.

The people in Nazareth said, "Isn't he the carpenter, the son of Mary?" (Mk. 6: 3). By the power of God, Mary had been chosen to be his mother and he grew up among these people. They are looking at their *Messiah*, but they reject him because they are spiritually blind and spiritually deaf.

Jesus makes reference here to himself when he says, that a 'Prophet' cannot be heard "in his own home town" (Mk. 6: 4). We also have reference to the *Servant* figure. "It was the will of the Lord that his *Servant* should grow like a plant taking root in dry ground" (Isaiah 53: 2).

It is interesting to note that although man fails to recognise the *Messiah*, evil spirits don't. "I know who you are – you are God's holy messenger" (Mk. 1: 24). Satan and Jesus had met before!

In Mark's Gospel Jesus uses the title *Son of Man* to identify himself. Sometimes the word is used as we would use the word 'I'.

"I will prove to you then, that the *Son of Man* has authority on earth" (Mk. 2: 10).

"For even the *Son of Man* did not come to be served but to serve" (Mk. 10: 45).

The *Son of Man* can be identified with the suffering Servant Messiah in Isaiah 53. We see the prophecy being fulfilled in Mark. "The *Son of Man* will suffer much and be rejected" (Mk. 9: 12). "The *Son of Man* will be handed over to men who will kill him" (Mk. 9: 31).

We have further reference to the *Son of Man* in Daniel. Daniel sees a vision of *Christ* and he was like a *Son of Man* (Daniel 7: 13-14) The people should know their scripture, but because Jesus is not their idea of the *Messiah*, it would never dawn on them. Jesus by using this title has given them a hint of his true identity, but they fail spiritually to see or hear. It is going to take time for those who will eventually believe, to understand the true meaning of *Messiahship*. Jesus treats the whole situation with great discretion. As the Gospel unfolds, so the disciples true understanding of *Messiahship* grows. After the Resurrection, a deeper understanding is accomplished. Let us now see how the titles *Son of God, Son of David* arise in the understanding of *Messiahship* and how the understanding of who Jesus really is, develops only very, very slowly!

After feeding the 5,000 Jesus is confronted with the fear that the disciples display in the boat. They fail to realise that there is no cause for fear, because they have the *Messiah* in their presence. So when Jesus heals the blind man at Bethsaida there is a spiritual message for the disciples. Notice that Jesus touches the blind man twice, when he could have healed him immediately with a look, one word or one touch. He is doing this for the benefit of his disciples' spirituality. He is saying that it will take time for their spiritual blindness to go, but that when it does they will see clearly and understand the meaning of true *Messiahship*. At the first touch the man only saw people like trees, he is only just aware of their presence. Now there are people who are only aware of 'self' and remain like that even after the first touch of Baptism. They do not want to know about other people's problems, but God said, "Love your neighbour" (Mk 12: 31). Because God is aware of our spiritual weakness He gives man a second anointing, Baptism of the Holy Spirit, to bring us into a deeper spiritual relationship. When Jesus touches the man a second time he sees clearly. Jesus is showing the disciples the fact that only very gradually are they beginning to realise who he is. Jesus lives with them, they experience his unique power and yet they are very slow to comprehend who he is.

Now we must look at what is called the 'turning point' in Mark's

Gospel. Jesus' ministry in Galilee is almost over and the journey to Jerusalem, his death on Calvary, is about to begin.

Jewish belief of the expected *Messiah* is based on the Sacred Scriptures which state, "He will rule as King David's successor," (Isaiah 9: 7) and "A day is coming when the new king from the royal line of David will be a symbol to the nations" (Isaiah 11: 10). The Jews are expecting an earthly king, one who will come with splendour and pomp. They are worldly people and will not accept Jesus, the humble Servant of his Father. If Jesus declares at the outset of his ministry that he is the *Christ*, the Jews will kill him for blasphemy, or the Romans will kill him for treason. This is why Jesus conceals his true identity. As Mark shows in his Gospel, the title *Messiah* has to unfold gradually until Jesus has accomplished his mission on earth. Jesus is not an earthly king; he is, as Mark portrays, God's Holy *Servant*. He is not a man of war, which he shows when he rides into Jerusalem on a colt. A man of peace will ride a colt and a man of war, an earthly king or soldier, will ride a horse.

On many occasions after a healing, or a miracle, we find Jesus telling the people not to mention what has occurred. We know the reason why. Jesus is being very discreet and he plays down the role of *Messiahship*.

"The evil spirits recognise him".

"He would not let the demons say anything because they knew who he was" (Mk. 1: 34) (Jesus heals many).

"Jesus sternly ordered the evil spirits not to tell anyone who he was" (Mk. 3: 12) (People with evil spirits).

"But Jesus gave them strict orders not to tell anyone" (Mk. 5: 43) (Healing of Jairus' daughter).

"Then Jesus ordered the people not to speak of it to anyone" (Mk. 7: 36) (Jesus heals a deaf mute).

"Don't tell anyone what you have seen" (Mk. 9: 9) (Transfiguration).

"Do not tell anyone about me" (Mk. 8: 30) (Caesarea Philippi).

"Don't go back to the village" (Mk. 8: 26) (Blind man of Bethsaida).

Nearing Caesarea Philippi Jesus asks, "Who do people say I am?" (Mk. 8: 27). Jesus is enquiring as to what impact his teaching has had on the people. Now the disciples have heard and seen enough of his teachings to know his true identity. Jesus says, "Who do you say I am?" (Mk. 8: 29). You will notice in the Gospel that Peter always speaks for the others. "You are the *Messiah*", (Mk. 8: 29) answered Peter. Jesus then gives them a true picture of the *Messiah* and tells them that the *Messiah* will fulfil the prophecy of Isaiah. "It was my will that he should suffer, his death was a sacrifice to bring forgiveness" (Isaiah 53: 10). This is too much for Peter. "So Peter took him aside and began to rebuke him" (Mk. 8: 32). Jesus rebukes Peter, "get away from me Satan. Your thoughts don't come from God but from man" (Mk. 8: 33). Jesus speaks like this because it is the only way to bring Peter back on to the spiritual level. Peter and the disciples still do not yet fully understand the true meaning of *Messiahship*.

Following this incident Jesus takes Peter, James and John up Mount Hermon. Here, he allows them to see his true identity and for a brief moment they will see the Divine Glory of God. This vision is very important, because Jesus knows that it will be extremely difficult for them to remember that he is the *Messiah* when they see him on Calvary. Jesus wants this experience to carry them through. "A change came over Jesus and his clothes became shining white – whiter than anyone in the world could wash them" (Mk. 9: 3). Human words, though Mark tries, will never describe the Glory of God.

When Peter puts Jesus on the same plain as Moses, who is the great lawgiver of the Old Testament and Elijah, who is the great prophet, God intervened. "This is my own dear *Son*, listen to him!" (Mk. 9: 7). God is saying look your *Messiah* is standing right in front of you!! The disciples look round because they are still spiritually blind! It is going to take time as Jesus had predicted.

It is interesting to note that after Jesus speaks to them about the *Passion*, they do not discuss what they will do when this horrific event takes place. They appear to be oblivious of his words and discuss who will be the greatest in God's Kingdom. Later, Jesus again speaks about his death. This is followed by James and John asking Jesus if they can sit on either side of his throne. This clearly shows that they do not understand the whole truth of Jesus' *Messiahship*. They are still growing spiritually. When Jesus is leaving Jericho, a blind beggar called Bartimaeus shouts out, "Jesus, *Son of David*" (Mk. 10: 47). Bartimaeus is the only person other than Peter to have called him the *Messiah*. As I said earlier, to the Jews, the *Messiah* would be a descendant of King David and to use the title *Son of David* meant *Messiah*.

In Mark chapter eleven we see Jesus in his first major role. He enters Jerusalem in fulfilment of the prophecy, "See now your *King* comes to you" (Zachariah 9: 9). When the people throw their cloaks down in front of the colt, it is a sign that they recognise that Jesus is claiming *Kingship*. People around begin to shout after Jesus "God bless the coming kingdom of *King David*, our *father!* (Mk. 11: 10).

If Jesus wants to claim an earthly *Kingship* he will go to the Fortress Antonia to take over from Pilate, or he will take over King Herod's palace. However Jesus goes straight to the temple, to his Father's house, for he is claiming a Spiritual Kingdom but the people do not understand this.

Anointing is the symbol of *Kingship* and *Death*. Now the woman who anoints Jesus at Bethany is anointing the body of Jesus before he dies. It is Wednesday of Holy Week, just before the night of his agony and he is going to suffer a most horrific death. Once you are condemned by the Romans to crucifixion, no honour is given to your body. The body is thrown to the wild animals. It is most exceptional that Jesus is even allowed to be buried. The bystanders, including Judas, according to John's Gospel, object strongly to the action of this woman. Jesus accepts, that the honour that is due to his body, as the *Son of God*, has been given it through this lady. "She poured perfume on my body to prepare it ahead of time for burial" (Mk. 14: 8).

The title *Son of God* is made recognisable by Jesus' unique power and authority shown throughout his ministry. There is also the deep and loving relationship between Jesus and his Father, which is expressed twice by the Father. "You are my own dear *Son*, I am pleased with you" (Mk. 1: 11) and "This is my own dear *Son*, listen to him" (Mk. 9: 7)

Finally the secret of *Messiahship* is brought into the open when the High Priest says, "Are you the *Messiah*, the *Son of the Blessed God*? (Mk. 14: 61). Jesus answered "*I am*" (Mk. 14: 62).

We are later to see the title, "*King of the Jews* (Mk. 15: 26). This is a notice nailed to the cross as a form of mockery. Standing by the cross is a Roman soldier who gives recognition of Jesus by stating, "This man was really the *Son of God*" (Mk. 15: 39).

The aim of Mark's Gospel is to reveal to the people of his time, who underwent great persecution and to the people of the present day, that the Good News that Jesus brings reveals that he is the *Son of God.*

OPPOSITION AND CONFLICT AGAINST JESUS AND HIS DISCIPLES

BLASPHEMY IN
FORGIVING SINS
2:V7

EATING WITH TAX
COLLECTORS AND
OUTCASTS
2:V16

NOT FASTING
2:V18
DISCIPLES

BREAKING THE
SABBATH LAW
2:V23
DISCIPLES

THE GREAT
COMMANDMENT
12:V28-34

EATING WITH
UNCLEAN
HANDS 7:V1-5
DISCIPLES

CASTING OUT
DEVILS BY
THE POWER
OF SATAN
3:V22

RISING
FROM THE
DEAD
12:V18-27

HEALING
ON THE
SABBATH
3:V1-5

DIVORCE
10:V2-12

If we accept the Kingship of God, this means we acknowledge Jesus as the *Messiah*, the *Son of Man* and accepting *God* as our *Father*, means acknowledging Jesus as the *Son of God*.

The question for all time and all men is, "Who do you say I am?"

Opposition and Conflict

Blasphemy

(Chapter 2: 1-12.)

Here the teachers of the law take their first stand against Jesus. Only God can forgive sins and so they accuse him of blasphemy. Jesus does not say that he is God, he only says, "My son, your sins are forgiven". The Scribes are spiritually blind and fail to see their Messiah standing in front of them.

Eating With Sinners

(Chapter 2: 13-17.)

To sit and have a meal with someone is a sign of friendship. The Pharisees cannot understand how Jesus can sit and eat with people that they consider to be sinners. It is totally against the Jewish law. The test that Jesus gives to the Pharisees is to admit that they are sinners, but they fail the test. They can only stand and criticise Jesus.

Fasting

(Chapter 2: 18-20.)

The followers of John the Baptist like the Pharisees fast on the second and fifth days of the week. They cannot understand why the disciples are not fasting. John the Baptist has referred to "The Bridegroom" in his teachings of the Messiah, (John 3:29) and now we have Jesus illustrating his answer by reference to a wedding feast. He is the Bridegroom of the New Israel and the disciples are his representatives. This wedding will produce the new wine of the Kingdom of God. Therefore whilst Jesus is with them they should rejoice and feast.

The Sabbath. Work

(Chapter 2: 23-28.)

The Pharisees are watching Jesus closely. They accuse his disciples, not Jesus, of breaking the law. To pluck the ears of corn is to reap and to rub the husks in one's hand is to thresh. This comes under their heading of work which is not allowed on the Sabbath. Jesus comes to their defence. Though he does not openly claim to be the Messiah, his authoritative answer in verse 27 must have left the Pharisees angry. For here is a claim to be greater than Moses, as Lord and Master of the Sabbath. Further, that the Sabbath is not to put man into slavery, but that it is created for man's good. He is saying that man's requirements are more important than their laws. The Jewish religion has gone far too legalistic. They have 613 rules for the Sabbath day alone.

The Sabbath. Healing

(Chapter 3: 1-6.)

Those who have hatred in their hearts for Jesus are watching him closely to see if he will break the law. The law only allowed cases of life or death to be treated on the Sabbath. These people already have premeditated murder in their hearts. They hope that Jesus will heal the man, for this will give them evidence against him. It also reflects the lack of love that they have for the sick. Jesus does not break the Sabbath law because he does not touch the man, but heals him by word. The people are made to look more unwise and stupid, when Jesus saysthat not to do good, when you have the power, is to do evil. In their hatred for Jesus, they go away to plot his murder.

Beelzbul Charge

(Chapter 3: 22)

The teachings and power that Jesus is displaying to the people are obviously causing concern for the teachers of the law. His popularity is drawing "large crowds" to him. This infuriates those who are against him. They want to destroy him and his reputation. So they accuse him of casting out demons by the power of the Devil. Jesus has already healed many people who are possessed with evil spirits. Jesus explains that it is ridiculous to believe that evil will cast out evil and that it is only by God's goodness that evil is cast out. He also explains to them that if countries and families allow evil to reside within themselves, they will destroy themselves. If anger, hatred, greed and other evils are allowed to grow in people's hearts the result will be destructive. Only by God's power and love are we freed from the destruction of Satan. Jesus illustrates this when he speaks of the strong man, for only God's power can tie up Satan and free man from evil.

Religious Cleanliness

(Chapter 7: 1-23.)

The Scribes and Pharisees even come from Jerusalem to spy on Jesus in the hope of getting evidence against him. On this occasion they find the disciples eating, as they judged, with *unclean* hands. Jewish law insists on the people washing their hands, even up to the elbow. Cooking and drinking utensils have to be washed in a special way. This is not done for hygienic reasons, but because the Jew might have been in contact with something that a gentile has touched. Therefore they will be *unclean* and should purify themselves. Do you see the sin of pride? They put themselves above everyone else. Jesus tells them that they are "hypocrites". Their rules and regulations have no meaning and therefore their worship is useless. Jesus quotes from Isaiah 29:13. He tells them that they have made a mockery of the commandments of God, by their own man-made rules. They have accused Jesus and his disciples of not keeping to the Law. Now Jesus in his great compassion only accuses them of breaking the fourth commandment. Indeed this is only one of many that they are breaking! Jesus explains that it is not what goes into the mouth of a man that makes him unclean, but rather what comes out of the mouth. The heart is the centre of all man's motivation and God wants man to have a new heart and a new spirit. God wants men to live good and loving lives and be obedient to his word.

You can imagine how the spirit of anger and hatred infused their hearts. They are so full of their own importance and superiority that they are blind to the truth.

The Teaching on Divorce

(Chapter 10: 1-12.)

There are two schools of thought concerning this question among the Jewish people. The school of Shammai belive that a marriage only comes to an end if the wife committes adultery. The penalty for such an act is death (Deut. 22:1). The school of Hillel believes that a husband can divorce his wife if she displeases him. The grounds for this are so trivial, in as much, that if she cooks a dinner that he does not enjoy, or says something that annoys him, he can just write a letter of divorce and tell her to leave (Deut. 24:1). They obviously want to test Jesus when they put this question to him. Jesus tells them that it is because they are so unteachable that Moses gave permission. He quotes from Gen. 2:24-25, telling them that marriage is God's idea and that it is a Holy and Sacred Bond.

The Question about Jesus' Authority

(Chapter 11:27-33.)

The religious leaders have come to challenge Jesus in the hope that they will trap him. They are frustrated and angry because they still have no evidence against him. Jesus in his great wisdom turns the question back on them. Though they know the true answer, they cannot say that the authority comes from 'God', because they do not listen to John's teachings and repent. They cannot say that it was by man's authority, because this will enrage the followers of John. These followers of John the Baptist believe that he has spoken by God's authority. The religious leaders by their very own *trap* have *trapped* themselves. It left them looking very foolish indeed!

The Question on Paying Taxes

(Chapter 12: 13-17.)

Some Pharisees and Herodians gather together in the hope of trapping Jesus with a political question. If he says **yes**, they will accuse him of being a traitor to his people, if he says **no**, they will hand him over to the authorities as a traitor. In his infinite wisdom he asks for a coin. The image of the Emperor is on the coin. So Jesus tells them to, "Pay what belongs to the Emperor". Yet there is a higher authority than the Emperor and that is God. The Emperor has been made in the image of God. So Jesus tells them to, "Pay God what belongs to God". In other words they must recognise human authority, but

God's authority must also be recognised. This answer must have truly shattered them.

A Question About Rising From Death
(Chapter 12: 18-27.)
This time they try to trap Jesus with a doctrinal question. The question comes from the Sadducees who do not believe in life after death, angels, or spirits. Jesus tells them that they do not know their scriptures and uses the word "when" not "if", in reference to the dead rising again. He has stated a fact! He explains that there will be no such thing as marriage because we will have spiritual bodies. The Sadducees are supposed to have great knowledge of the scriptures and have taken their question from the law of Moses though the interpretation is of their own making. If Jesus disagrees with the law of Moses then they will have reason to find fault with him. Jesus explains that there is life after death. He reminds them of when God said to Moses, "I am", in the present tense, "The God of Abraham, Isaac and Jacob". Now they have been dead over four hundred years, but here Jesus is telling them that they are spiritually alive! Therefore God is the God of the living. Their own ignorance must have left them humiliated and frustrated.

The Greatest Commandment
(Chapter 12: 28-34.)
A teacher of the law put another question to him. It is incredible to imagine, after all they have seen and heard, that they will dare to test his knowledge. There are 613 laws, some are moral laws and others are ceremonial laws. They want the impossible, an answer in a sentence. Only someone exceedingly special to God could have given them the answer. The Son of God answers them by reciting the Shema. This is the daily Jewish prayer and the word 'Shema' is the Hebrew for 'hear' (Deut. 6:4-6). Jesus links this by quoting from Leviticus 19:18. So they have their answer. Firstly they must love God and secondly their neighbour. For the first time one of the teachers of the law can see the wisdom behind the words that Jesus speaks and he praises his answer.

Note
For more detail on the above headings consult the chapters.

Suggested Questions for Course Work

Knowledge

1. Choose five occasions when people recognised that Jesus was a very special person in Mark's Gospel.

2. Select one example in each case, from Mark's Gospel, where Jesus met opposition from:

   a) teachers of the law
   b) Pharisees
   c) respect for civil authority

3. Choose a passage from Mark's Gospel to illustrate:

   a) the calling of the disciples
   b) the loyalty of the disciples
   c) the weakness of the disciples
      in their following of Jesus

4. Give three examples from Mark's Gospel where Jesus offended against Jewish belief or religious custom.

5. Re-tell the story of the parable that explains that man should put his security in God and not in materialism.

Understanding

1. Peter's reply to Jesus' question at Caesarea Philippi, "Who do you say I am?" is often seen as the turning point of Mark's Gospel.

   Explain carefully why you think this is so.

2. a) Why was Jesus critical of the Jewish laws and traditions at that time?

   b) How did Jesus show the power of good over evil?

   c) Why did Jesus reply in the way he did to the question concerning the paying of taxes in Mark 12?

3. Explain how Christians try to put into practice the ideal of Jesus, concerning way of life, money, and talents.

4. Why did Jesus use a child to illustrate the qualities of discipleship?

5. Explain in your own words the parable of the sower.

Evaluation

1. In what way is the Baptism of the Holy Spirit (*Confirmation*) important in the life of a young Christian today.

2. Do you think there are situations in the world today where conflict may arise for Christians between loyalty to Christ's teaching and human authority?
   Give reasons for your answer.

3. Being a disciple can be very costly for the individual.
   Why do you think it is worth the sacrifice?
   Illustrate with examples.

4. In the world today we have hunger, poverty, and disease.

   a) Why do you think these problems exist?

   b) Do you think that other countries and individuals have a responsibility to help those less fortunate than themselves?

   Give reasons for your answer.

5. How do you think Christians today interpret the Second Coming of Jesus? What evidence is given of the Second Coming in Mark's Gospel?

Questions

Question 1.
Which three disciples were with Jesus when he was transfigured?

(a)　1.
　　　2.
　　　3.

(b) Name the two men from the Old Testament who appeared with Jesus in the Transfiguration. State who represented the law, and who represented the prophets.

　　　1.
　　　2.

(c) What name did Jesus give to the disciples James and John?

　　　1.
　　What was their father's name?
　　　2.

(d) Which disciple was a Zealot

　　　1.
　　What did this group hope to obtain?
　　　2.
　　Which disciple was a tax collector?
　　　3.

(e) Why do you think Jesus chose *twelve* disciples?
　　　1.

Question 2

(a) What did Jesus say about the Sabbath?
   1.

(b) On which two occasions did Jesus heal on the Sabbath?
   1.
   2.

(c) Name an occasion when Jesus came into conflict with the Pharisees over the Sabbath.
   1.

(d) Which day of the week do the Jews keep as their Sabbath?
   1.

(e) What event in Mark's Gospel made Sunday the Holy Day for Christians?
   1.

Question 3

(a) "You are God's Holy Messenger." What does messenger mean?
   1.
   Who said this?
   2.

(b) "This man has authority."
   What does authority mean in this situation?
   1.

(c) Name another occasion when Jesus showed authority over evil spirits.
   1.

(d) What other name did Satan have in Mark's Gospel?
   1.

(e) What does blasphemy mean?
   1.

Question 4

(a) What is the name of the festival when Pilate freed a prisoner?
    1.

(b) When Jesus died what did the army officer say?
    1.

(c) What does Golgotha mean?
    1.

(d) Who asked Pilate for the body of Jesus?
    1.

(e) What does "Eloi, Eloi, lema Sabachthani" mean?
    1.

(f) What language is this?
    1.

Question 5

(a) What does exorcism mean?
    1.

(b) What did Jesus say was very necessary for exorcism?
    1.

(c) Name two healing miracles which involved exorcism.
    1.
    2.

(d) Name a miracle performed by
    1. Touch
    2. Words

(e) Name a miracle of faith healed from a distance.
    1.

(f) Name three nature miracles.
    1.
    2.
    3.

Question 6

(a) What did Jesus say to the paralysed man that made the teachers of the law angry?
    1.

(b) In which miracle is Jesus called the 'Son of David'?
    1.

(c) In which miracle did Jesus speak sternly to the sick person?
    1.

(d) Where did Jesus heal the man with the paralysed hand?
    1.

Question 7

(a) What is a parable?
    1.

(b) What is an allegory?
    1.

(c) Name the four kinds of soil in the Parable of the Sower.
    1.
    2.
    3.
    4.

(d) Name two parables that are also allegories.
    1.
    2.

(e) Name two parables that speak about the growth of the Kingdom.
    1.
    2.

(f) Name a parable that shows that God will be our judge.
    1.

(g) Name a parable which states that Judaism is dead.
   1.

(h) Name a parable that speaks about the New Covenant.
   1.

(j) Why do you think Jesus spoke in parables?
   1.

Question 8

(a) Explain the allegorical meaning of the 'Sower' in Mark's Gospel.

(b) In the parable of the Rich Young Man
   1. Explain why he failed to follow Jesus.
   2. Explain Jesus' teaching on riches and entering the
      Kingdom of God.

(c) Explain two parables that teach us about the Kingdom
    of God.

Question 9

(a) What do you understand by the title "Son of Man".

(b) What do you understand by the title "Son of God".

(c) What do you understand by the title "Son of David".

(d) How did the people in Nazareth respond to Jesus?

Question 10

(a) What did Jesus say in Mark's Gospel about:-
   1. Marriage
   2. Divorce

(b) 1. What was Jesus' native language?
     2. Give two examples from Mark's Gospel.

(c) 1. Of what importance is Mark's Gospel in our lives today?

Illustrate from the Gospel in your answers.

(d) What do you understand by 'The Kingdom of God'?